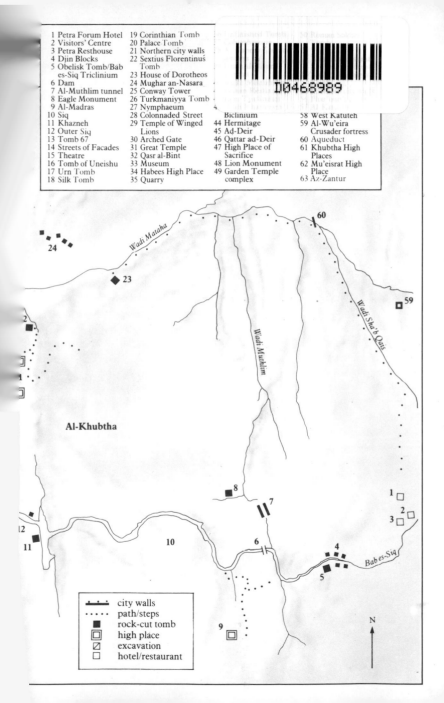

1 Petra Forum Hotel
2 Visitors' Centre
3 Petra Resthouse
4 Djin Blocks
5 Obelisk Tomb/Bab es-Siq Triclinium
6 Dam
7 Al-Muthlim tunnel
8 Eagle Monument
9 Al-Madras
10 Siq
11 Khazneh
12 Outer Siq
13 Tomb 67
14 Streets of Facades
15 Theatre
16 Tomb of Uneishu
17 Urn Tomb
18 Silk Tomb
19 Corinthian Tomb
20 Palace Tomb
21 Northern city walls
22 Sextius Florentinus Tomb
23 House of Dorotheos
24 Mughar an-Nasara
25 Conway Tower
26 Turkmaniyya Tomb
27 Nymphaeum
28 Colonnaded Street
29 Temple of Winged Lions
30 Arched Gate
31 Great Temple
32 Qasr al-Bint
33 Museum
34 Habees High Place
35 Quarry

Biclinium
44 Hermitage
45 Ad-Deir
46 Qattar ad-Deir
47 High Place of Sacrifice
48 Lion Monument
49 Garden Temple complex

58 West Katuteh
59 Al-Wu'eira Crusader fortress
60 Aqueduct
61 Khubtha High Places
62 Mu'eisrat High Place
63 Az-Zantur

Al-Khubtha

	city walls
.....	path/steps
■	rock-cut tomb
▣	high place
◩	excavation
□	hotel/restaurant

N

PETRA

A guide to the capital of the Nabataeans

Rami G Khouri

With photographs by the author

Longman

LONDON AND NEW YORK

**To the memory of
Elias and Salma Kettaneh**

LONGMAN GROUP UK LIMITED,
Longman House, Burnt Mill, Harlow,
Essex CM20 2JE, England
and Associated Companies throughout the world.

First published 1986

British Library Cataloguing in Publication Data

Khouri, Rami G.
Petra: a guide to the capital of the
Nabataeans.
1. Petra (Ancient city)
I. title
915.695'7   DA154.9.P48

ISBN 0-582-78385-2

Set in 11/11 Palatino Lasercomp

Produced by Longman Group (FE) Ltd
Printed in Hong Kong

Table of Contents

4

Author's Preface and Acknowledgements

This book has been designed and written to serve as a guide for those who wish seriously to explore Petra on their own. It takes ten to twelve full days to see everything of interest in the Petra area, though you can see the most important monuments in two or three. I hope this book will encourage residents of Jordan or of the region to return to Petra frequently, visiting a different area of the city on each trip.

On a practical note, I suggest that first trips to distant corners of the Petra basin (such as Sabra or Nebi Haroon) be attempted only with a guide or with someone who has made the trip before. When using this book, it is best to read about the area you plan to visit before setting out, to be aware of what to look for on the way. If you wander away from the city centre, stay near the tracks to avoid getting lost. On the other hand, one of the pleasures of visiting Petra is to strike out on an aimless stroll into one of the many small or large wadis that criss-cross the Petra region. Wherever you head, you will invariably come across fascinating and mysterious ancient monuments, water works or other installations that always challenge you to guess their original function. There is still much to be discovered and documented at Petra, and one of the thrills that any visitor can experience is to come across an inscription, a niche or a monument that has not been previously recorded.

In writing this book, I have drawn on the experience, knowledge, kindness and generosity of many people who have been associated with Petra in one way or another. I have tried always in the text to acknowledge the original research and ideas of the many scholars who have worked at Petra during the past century; my own, more modest, contribution tries to bring together the work of the archaeologists and historians into a single book that makes the fruit of their work easily accessible to the modern visitor. I am glad, however, to have this opportunity to thank a handful of friends whose invaluable help I have very much appreciated. They include Dr Adnan Hadidi, Director of Antiquities of the Hashemite Kingdom of Jordan; Petra Inspector

6

of Antiquities, Inyazi Shabaan; Rawya Nabil, Hanan al-Kurdi and the staff of the Department of Antiquities' Registration Centre; Peter Parr, Dr Philip C. Hammond, Dr Nabil Khairy, Dr Axel Knauf and Dr Fawzi Zayadine; Bill Eve, Alfonz Maloschik, Karl Hala, Abboud Jada and the rest of the management and staff of the Petra Forum Hotel; Adnan Mufti and his colleagues at the JETT bus company; Ali Khalaf and Hweimil Ali; and Dr Andrew Garrard and his colleagues at the British Institute at Amman for Archaeology and History. They and many others have all been extraordinarily helpful to me, for which I am most grateful. Working with David Royle, Janice Paveley and Andy Smart at Longmans has been, as always, a pleasure.

The transliteration of the Arabic place names has been done in a totally informal and non-academic manner, designed primarily to help the non-Arabic speaker to pronounce the names as closely as possible to their correct Arabic pronunciation.

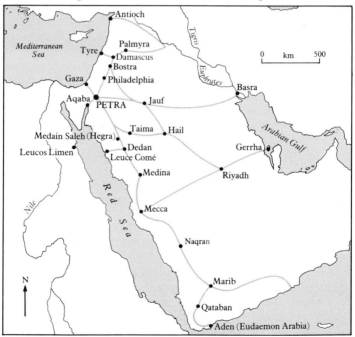

Trade routes in the Middle East in the Nabataean era

PART ONE

Visiting Petra: practical information and suggested itineraries

Accommodation

There are two sleeping/dining facilities at Petra. The Petra Forum Hotel, owned by the Jordanian government and managed by the Forum Hotels division of Intercontinental Hotels, has set new standards of comfort and service for tourist sites in Jordan since it opened in 1983. Reservations can be made through any Intercontinental or Forum hotel, or directly with the hotel (telex 64001, or telephone Amman 634200 or Wadi Musa 61246/7).

More budget-minded travellers might stay at the Petra Resthouse, owned and operated by the Tourist Investment Department of the Social Security Corporation. Reservations can be made through the Tourist Investment Department in Amman (telex 21607, telephone 813243/4/5), or directly with the Petra Resthouse (telephone Wadi Musa 11).

Visitors should note that it is now forbidden to sleep inside the ancient city, except with the prior written permission of the Department of Antiquities in Amman (telephone 644336). The office of the Petra Inspector of Antiquities is located in the old Nazzal's Camp building inside Petra, next to Qasr al-Bint (telephone Wadi Musa 6117).

Visitors' Centre

The Visitors' Centre at Petra is the usual starting place for a tour of the city. It is the headquarters of the government-appointed Tourist Police, who are always willing to be of service, answer questions or receive complaints. Government-trained guides are available at the Visitors' Centre. The Centre offers a wide range of basic services, including a bank, post office, restrooms, souvenirs, hats, postcards, films, books and brochures, and several showcases with artefacts from the Petra excavations. Note that it is forbidden by Jordanian law to buy or sell antiquities. All the souvenirs displayed and sold in the Petra region are modern copies of ancient artefacts. Jordanian law allows you to keep anything you may pick off the surface of the ground, such as pottery sherds, but it is strictly forbidden to break the surface of the ground in search of archaeological artefacts.

Transport
There are several ways to reach Petra from Amman, the usual entry point into Jordan for foreign visitors. The JETT bus company operates a daily round-trip bus tour to Petra from Amman, departing at 7.00 a.m. and returning at 7.00 p.m. You can rent a car and drive yourself to Petra, though for some this is a tiring day trip that requires nearly seven hours of driving. There are service (pronounced *servees*) taxis that operate regularly between Amman and Wadi Musa, the modern village next to Petra. A passenger in a service cab pays only for his own seat, and shares the fare with three or four other passengers.

SUGGESTED ITINERARIES

A three-day trip
The best way to visit Petra is to rent a car in Amman, leave at 7.00 a.m., and spend a full day on the Kings' Highway to Petra, breaking for lunch at the Crusader castle at Kerak. The second day, enter Petra early in the morning and visit the monuments along the Wadi Musa path in the city centre and the Royal Tombs, before breaking for lunch at the Forum Restaurant. After lunch, make the three-hour round-trip to Ad-Deir, returning to your hotel in the late afternoon. On the third day, enter Petra at dawn (8.00 a.m. in the colder days of winter), hike up to the High Place of Sacrifice, take the Wadi Farasa route down to the Qasr al-Bint area, and return to the hotel around 3.00 p.m. for lunch, a quick swim and the drive back to Amman.

A two-day trip
If you have only two days, leave Amman at 6.00 a.m. and drive straight to Petra on the Desert Highway (approximately three

hours), entering the city around 9.30 a.m. to catch the morning sun striking the facade of the Khazneh. Visit the city centre, the Royal Tombs, the Museum, the Habees High Place and the Habees Crusader Castle, returning to the hotel just before sunset. The second day, enter Petra at sunrise and climb to the High Place of Sacrifice (ideally, having breakfast at the High Place sent ahead by the Petra Forum Hotel). Return via the Wadi Farasa route to the Qasr al-Bint, and back through the city centre to the hotel for lunch and the drive back to Amman.

A one-day trip

The easiest way to make a return trip to Petra in the same day is to take the JETT bus tour, which gives you approximately three hours in Petra, including lunch and a guided tour. Should you wish to see more in a single day, you should rent a car and drive yourself. Leave Amman at dawn, arriving in Petra at around 9.00 a.m., and go straight into the city. After the Khazneh and the Outer Siq, climb the trail to the High Place of Sacrifice, and return via the Wadi Farasa to the area of Qasr al-Bint. Stop for lunch and a rest at the Forum Restaurant, and see the city centre, the Royal Tombs and the Theatre on your way back to the Visitors' Centre. Depart for Amman at 4.00 p.m., arriving around 7.00 p.m.

PART TWO

A historical introduction to the land of Edom, the Nabataean Kingdom, Petra and the Roman Province of Arabia

Petra's ancient prominence was due to the combination of its easily defended position, secure water resources, rich agricultural and grazing lands in the immediate vicinity, and a geographically strategic position near the junction of two of the ancient world's most important trade routes. The silk and spice routes that linked China, India and Southern Arabia with Rome and the Mediterranean world passed less than twenty kilometres to the east of Petra. From Petra, an established land route via the Wadi Araba, Gaza, and the north Sinai coast allowed men and goods to pass westwards to Egypt, through the formidable natural obstacles of mountains, inland seas, swamps and deserts that acted as a barrier between the eastern and western parts of the ancient Middle East.

While trade provided the economic base for the development of Petra into a splendid royal capital during the late Hellenistic era, the Petra basin area may first have been revered by the Nabataeans, in their early days in southern Jordan, as the sacred precinct of their god Dushara. The name Dushara means 'He of Sharra', referring to the Sharra mountains located north of Petra, and visible from it. It is possible that this sacred precinct was first used as a Nabataean necropolis, before becoming a magnificent capital city by the 1st century BC.

Even before the historical period, however, the Petra region was inhabited by Stone Age people who exploited its natural vegetation and wildlife. Diana Kirkbride's pioneering work at Beidha has revealed the presence of an important Neolithic village from the 7th millennium BC, along with traces of even earlier Natufian camps from the 9th and 10th millennia BC. Recent surveys and excavations in the Petra area by a West German team from Tubingen University, headed by Hans Peter Uerpmann and Hans Georg Gebel, have discovered a handful of new settlements, seasonally occupied campsites and rock shelters from the same closing millennia of the Stone Age.

EDOM AND THE NABATAEANS

The land of Edom in south Jordan has not received the attention of archaeologists and historians that it deserves. This was a strategic border and transit zone that was disputed among the diverse civilisations that encircled it from all sides throughout history, such as Egypt, Assyria, Mesopotamia, Persia, Judaea, Phoenicia, Greece, Rome, Byzantium and the Islamic nation. Internationally, the land of Edom sits like a pivot astride one of the great trade routes of the ancient world, linking the exotic commodity-producing regions of China, India and Southern Arabia with the rich, almost insatiable, markets of Rome, the Mediterranean lands, Egypt and Syria–Palestine.

The Nabataeans made their appearance in Jordan during the closing centuries of the Iron Age, roughly corresponding to the Old Testament period of the Bible. During the Iron Age (1200–333 BC), people came together to form more formidable, veritable little 'nations' that endured because of their higher level of political, economic, social and military organisation. Invariably kingdoms under a single, hereditary ruler, or confederations of tribes that may have rotated political leadership, these new 'nation-states' in Jordan included (from south to north) Edom, Moab, and Ammon, alongside neighbouring powers in Judaea and Phoenicia, among others.

The Assyrian Kingdom, from its base in the middle reaches of the Tigris and Euphrates rivers, dominated the smaller kingdoms of the Fertile Crescent and the eastern Mediterranean during most of the 8th and 7th centuries BC. Assyrian influence in southern Jordan has been shown clearly in the excavations of Mrs Crystal-M. Bennett at the two important Edomite towns of

Tawilan and Buseira, both of which can be visited today near Petra.

In 612 BC, the Babylonians and Chaldeans ended Assyrian hegemony in Jordan–Palestine, and threatened the small kingdoms in Edom, Moab and Ammon that had flourished as autonomous vassal states under Assyrian control. In the first two decades of the 6th century BC, the Babylonian King Nebuchadnezzar attacked and subjugated the Judaean, Ammonite and Moabite kingdoms; Edom followed soon after. Some scholars believe the Babylonian King Nabonidus (555–539 BC) was the one who finally brought Edom under Babylonian control, during his military campaigns in south Jordan and north Arabia in 552 BC. The Babylonian administration of Edom must have been relatively brief, for the Persian Cyrus conquered Arabia around 546–540 BC, before moving on to destroy Babylon in 539 BC. The Persian period in the history of Edom is one of the least known, for there are few historical references to it and even fewer inscriptions or excavations. It was during the historically turbid 7th-6th centuries BC that political control of the land of Edom passed successively from Edomite, to Assyrian, to Babylonian, and finally to Persian hands. This created the kind of intermittent instability that paved the way for a new group of people to stake a claim to the land and make of themselves a new regional power. These were the Arab people or tribe known as the Nabataeans.

The little hard historical evidence available today indicates they may have started to move into the land of Edom from northern Arabia some time in the early decades of the 6th century BC. As the Nabataeans gradually penetrated Edom from the south, the remnants of the now politically battered Edomites migrated westwards, into the southern reaches of the former Kingdom of Judaea. There, they established a new Edomite homeland called Edomea, better known by its Greek name of Idumea. The evidence suggests this was a gradual and peaceful process, which probably included considerable integration and cultural continuity between the Edomites and Nabataeans. There are several early historical references to Arab peoples whom scholars have tried to identify with the Nabataeans. The Assyrian records during the 8th–6th centuries BC mention Aramaic and/or Arab people called the 'Nabatu', the 'Nabaiateans', or the 'Na-ba-a-a-ti', and speak of 'the country of the Nabaieteans' and 'Natnu, king of the Nabai'ati'. The Old Testament speaks of the 'Nabaioth', while an inscription from Tayma mentions the 'nbyt' people. Most scholars now agree that none of these ancient references can be identified explicitly with the Nabataeans of Petra. The Nabataeans referred to themselves as 'Nabatu'.

We know with relative certainty that the Nabataeans were a nomadic Arab tribe from northern Arabia, who may have derived from the greater Qedarite tribal confederation that covered the area of southern Syria/northern Arabia, linked by the Wadi Sirhan stretches of east Jordan in between. According to some scholars, such as Dr Axel Knauf, there is geographical and linguistic evidence associating the Nabataeans with the Qedarites, the most powerful Arabian tribe in this area between the 8th and 5th centuries BC. By the 4th century BC, if not earlier, the Nabataeans had emerged as an independent and politically powerful tribe. They spoke an Arabic dialect, and by the late 4th century BC had adopted the more common Aramaic script which had become the *lingua franca* of the area under Persian rule, especially for commercial transactions. The generally accepted view is that they first moved into the land of Edom during the 6th–4th centuries BC, elbowed out the Edomites, and established their base at Petra by the 4th century BC. They prospered at first from livestocking, trade with southern Arabia, and extracting bitumen from the Dead Sea for export to Egypt. Certainly, there was a Nabataean settlement at Petra by the end of the 4th century BC, when we have the first fixed historical reference to them.

This comes from the *Bibliothieca* of the Sicilian historian Diodorus Siculus, who wrote during the 1st century BC. He based his work on the eye-witness accounts of Hieronymus of Cardia, a Greek military officer who served in the area at the end of the 4th century BC. Diodorus recounts the campaigns against the Nabataeans by the ruler of Syria, Antigonus ('the One-Eyed'), one of the more ambitious of Alexander the Great's former generals. In 312 BC, or about a decade after the death of Alexander, Antigonus sent a force of 4000 foot soldiers and 600 cavalry, under the command of an officer named Athenaeus, to attack the Nabataean Arabs and plunder their animals. Athenaeus had heard that the Arabs celebrated a national festival or fair every year, during which their women, children and possessions were left behind in safety on the summit of a 'strong but unwalled rock'. This rock has always been equated with Umm al-Biyara, the mountain that dominates the central Petra basin from the west. Excavations have shown the presence of an Edomite settlement on the summit of Umm al-Biyara, with possible Hellenistic occupation and substantial Nabataean remains.

Athenaeus approached Umm al-Biyara from the west, and attacked during the cover of night, when all the men were attending their national gathering (probably an annual or seasonal commercial fair). The Greeks sacked the place, killed and imprisoned some of the Arab population, and returned to the west with booty that included 'about 500 talents of silver', and most of the frankincense and myrrh the Nabataeans had stored. The Nabataeans gave chase, caught up with the attackers, and killed Athenaeus and all but fifty of his troops, who escaped. Back home at Petra, the Nabataeans sent a diplomatic letter of complaint to Antigonus (written 'in Syrian characters', or Aramaic), and the humiliated Antigonus replied with more diplomacy than truth that the attack was an unfortunate excess on the part of Athenaeus, who had disregarded orders and acted on his own. It was a transparent lie, for Antigonus wanted the financial gain that came from control of the trade routes in the land of Edom, and soon after sent his son Demetrius 'the Besieger' (or 'the conqueror of cities') to attack the Nabataeans once again. The Nabataeans caught early sight of the invasion force and alerted the garrison at Petra, who scattered their coveted flocks of cattle, fortified the rock, and thus prevented a Greek attack. Nabataean precaution seems to have been followed by successful oratory, for Diodorus says that a moving speech by one of the Nabataean elders convinced the Greeks that the Nabataeans were not like them, in that they did not build houses, drink wine, or grow fruit trees or wheat, and only wanted to live in peace with them and would never become their slaves. After some negotiations, Demetrius consented to the Nabataean offer of gifts and some hostages, and retreated towards the Dead Sea.

Diodorus portrays the Nabataeans at the end of the 4th century BC as a nomadic people who valued their flocks and shunned built houses and cultivation that required a long stay in one place; they traded in frankincense and myrrh, were capable of writing in some form of Aramaic, and preferred negotiated compromises to military confrontations with their enemies. This valuable early portrait of the Nabataeans' life and culture is then followed by a relatively long gap in credible historical reports about them, punctuated only by isolated references to the Nabataeans in different parts of the Middle East. Evidence from papyrus documents in the archive of Zenon of Caunus, in Egypt, proves the Nabataeans were in the Hauran region of southern Syria by 259 BC, and refers to 'Rabbel', a common Nabataean royal name. A King Rabbel I may have reigned in the second half of the 2nd century BC. Diodorus' accounts mention that towards the end of the 3rd century BC there were 'many inhabited villages of Arabs who are known as Nabataeans. This tribe occupies a large part of the coast and not a little of the country which stretches inland, and it has a people numerous beyond telling and flocks and herds in multitude beyond belief . . .' The earliest known Nabataean inscription comes from Elusa, along the important Petra–Gaza road in the Naqab (Negev). It reads: 'This is the place which Nuthairu made for the life of Aretas, king of the Nabataeans.' The Abbé Starcky dates this inscription on paleographic grounds to the first half of the 2nd century BC, making it the earliest known reference to the Nabataean monarchy.

There are several biblical references to the Nabataeans in the Books of Maccabees, referring to events that took place during the middle of the 2nd century BC. One passage, dated to 169/168 BC, mentions 'Aretas the prince of the Arabians', a reference to Aretas I, the first Nabataean king we know of. Diodorus then reports that the Nabataeans' . . . not only attacked the shipwrecked, but fitting out pirate ships preyed upon the voyagers . . .; some time afterwards, however, they were caught on the high seas by some quadriremes and punished as they deserved'.

This report of Nabataean piracy, probably on the Red Sea, is corroborated by the Roman writer Strabo. Professor Glen Bowersock has suggested that the Nabataeans may have resorted to piracy during the 2nd and 1st centuries BC, when their control of the trade routes – and therefore their very livelihood – was threatened by the discovery of the monsoon winds. This permitted the establishment of direct sea routes between India, southern Arabia, Egypt and the Mediterranean, thereby providing an alternative to the overland trade routes that passed through Petra. This would have generated some fierce competition between the Nabataeans and the powers of Ptolemaic Egypt, resulting perhaps in the Nabataeans' drastic resort to piracy, only to be badly mauled by the Ptolemaic navy.

From the 1st century BC, generally reliable historical references to the Nabataeans become more plentiful. Around the year 100 BC, according to the historian Josephus, the Jewish Hasmonaean leader Alexander Jannaeus besieged the people of Gaza; they in turn anticipated in vain that 'Aretas, the King of the Arabs, would come to their assistance', perhaps on the assumption that the Nabataeans could not afford to allow an important export/transit port such as Gaza to fall into hostile hands. This is thought to be a reference to the Nabataean King Aretas II, the first Nabataean monarch to issue his own coins. He seems to have reigned during a time of Nabataean expansion, taking advantage of in-fighting among the Seleucids after 129 BC.

Aretas II was probably succeeded by his son, Obodas I, who inherited both the monarchy and an adversarial relationship with the Jewish Hasmonaeans. Obodas I may have been succeeded by a King Rabbel I, but the next firmly identified Nabataean monarch was the son of Obodas I, King Aretas III (86–62 BC), who continued the decades-old Nabataean thrust to the north. Invited by the people of Damascus to save them from the threatening Ituraean kingdom in the area of modern Lebanon, Aretas III took over Damascus around 84 BC and ruled it through an appointed governor for over a dozen years. The Armenian King Tigranes took Damascus soon after 72 BC, and the Nabataeans retreated peacefully. Tigranes himself vacated Damascus in 69 BC to deal with a Roman threat against his own capital. This power vacuum in Damascus and the rest of Syria paved the way for the entry onto the Middle Eastern stage of a decisive new power that would determine the fate of the area for many centuries: the Roman General Pompey captured Damascus in 64 BC, and reorganised the area into the new Roman Province of Syria.

The widow of Alexander Jannaeus, Alexandra, had died in 67 BC, sparking a fight for power between her sons Hyrcanus II and Aristobulus. Hyrcanus lost a major battle against his brother's forces at Jericho, fled, and found refuge at Petra, the capital city of the Nabataean King Aretas III. Pompey probably planned to deal with the Nabataeans in a manner that would at least neutralise them – through war or peaceful treaty – and avert any possible military threat from the area south of the Decapolis and the

Province of Syria. But the feud among the rulers in Jerusalem deflected his attention away from Nabataea, and in 63 BC he personally took control of Jerusalem and returned Hyrcanus to power. Pompey returned to Rome in 62 BC, having left the area in the hands of the first governor of Syria, Aemilius Scaurus. He lost no time in sending a military force against the Nabataeans, but fighting was averted, negotiations and reason prevailed, and the Romans withdrew after accepting Aretas III's offer of 300 talents of silver. The Nabataeans thus secured a working accommodation with the power of Rome to the north, and a continuation of their vital trading activity. Around 60 BC, Aretas III died and was succeeded by King Malichus I, though there is considerable scholarly debate about when this transition took place, and about the possibility of a King Obodas II having reigned briefly between 62 and 58 BC.

In 40 BC, Parthian forces from Iran reached Jerusalem, as part of the complex battles for power among Roman leaders, and gained Malichus' support. The Jewish leader Herod left Jerusalem and unsuccessfully sought refuge with Malichus at Petra, after which he travelled to Rome to press his claim as leader of the Jewish Kingdom. Herod was installed by Rome as King of Judaea, and returned triumphantly to evict the Parthians from Jerusalem in 39 BC, subsequently forcing Malichus and others who had supported the Parthians to pay 'large sums of money'. Herod and the Nabataeans went on to have several more military clashes in the following decade.

Malichus died in 30 BC, after more than three decades in power, and was succeeded by King Obodas II (30–9 BC). Rome formally annexed Egypt the same year, after the deaths of Antony and Cleopatra. A period of considerable regional political intrigues followed, which resulted in a battle between the Jewish forces of Herod and the Nabataeans of Obodas in 9 BC. During the winter of 9–8 BC, King Obodas died. He was succeeded by the greatest of Nabataean kings, a certain Aeneas who was to rule from 9 BC to AD 40 as Aretas IV, 'the lover of his people'.

In AD 6, Rome annexed Judaea and created the Province of Judaea, which, with the previous Roman annexations of Egypt and Syria, once again provided the regional stability that allowed trade to flourish and the Nabataeans to enter their era of greatest development. To make relations with Judaea even better, the Jewish leader Herod Antipas married a daughter of Aretas. The next several decades saw the sudden blossoming of the Nabataean city at Medain Saleh (Hegra), in northern Arabia, a key stop on the trade route from southern Arabia. Nabataean cities in southern Syria and the Negev also prospered and grew, and the Nabataean realm now included southern Syria, the Negev and Sinai deserts, the entire Wadi Sirhan basin in east Jordan, and the area of northern Arabia between Hegra and Aqaba. The capital at Petra, with a population estimated at 20–30,000, was the showcase of Nabataean prosperity and pride. Aretas IV died in AD 40, and was succeeded by his son, Malichus II, who continued for a time to oversee the growth of the Nabataean realm that his father had established.

The Roman writer Strabo, writing in the early 1st century AD about events around the end of the 1st century BC, left a detailed account of Nabataean culture at that time. He writes of

'Nabataea, a country with a large population and well supplied with pasturage ... The Nabataeans are a sensible people, and are so much inclined to acquire possessions that they publicly fine anyone who has diminished his possessions and also confer honours on anyone who has increased them ... they prepare common meals together in groups of thirteen persons ... The king holds many drinking-bouts in magnificent style, but no one drinks more than eleven cupfuls, each time using a different golden cup. The king is so democratic that, in addition to serving himself, he sometimes even serves the rest himself in turn ... Their homes, through the use of stone, are costly; but on account of peace, the cities are not walled... The sheep are white-fleeced and the oxen are large, but the country produces no horses. Camels render service in their places ...'

Strabo also mentions the presence of Romans and other foreigners at Petra, by then a magnificent city with active courts of laws, well endowed with water and gardens, and full of imported goods. The reign of Malichus II (AD 40–70), though long, is not well documented, for his reign left behind few coins or inscriptions. Certainly, as Starcky and others have pointed out, his reign saw increasing sedentarisation by his people, particularly in the northern parts of the kingdom, in the Hauran. Malichus II died in 70 and was succeeded by Rabbel II (70–106), whose mother, Queen Shuqailat, acted as regent for a few years until he came of age and assumed power. He was the last independent Nabataean king, and it was he who transferred the Nabataean capital from Petra to Bostra, in southern Syria. This partly reflected the shift in the trade routes that saw more goods bypassing Petra, moving instead by sea from Southern Arabia to Egypt, or over inland routes that went through the Wadi Sirhan or even via Palmyra. An inscription from Oboda in the Negev refers to Rabel II as 'King of the Nabataeans, who brought life and deliverance to his people'.

THE ROMAN ERA

Rabbel II's death in 106, combined with a possible decline in the former power of the Nabataean Kingdom, may have given Rome the opening it sought to move on this independent Arab power that nestled amidst its own provinces in Egypt, Judaea and Syria. In 106 the Roman Emperor Trajan ordered the governor of Syria to move south and conquer the Nabataeans. On 22 March 106 the Nabataean Kingdom came to an end, and the era of Roman control began. The Romans reorganised the area of Jordan–Syria by establishing a new Province of Arabia in the south, alongside the Province of Syria to the north. The new province, *Provincia Arabia*, included some of the former cities of the Decapolis, such as Gerasa (Jerash) and Philadelphia (Amman), Petra itself, and most of the former Nabataean kingdom. Bostra was designated as the capital of the new province. Trajan gave Petra the title of *metropolis* in 114, indicating that it remained an important urban centre even though it had lost the glamour that came with being the regional capital. Much archaeological evidence from Petra itself indicates that the Roman occupation and annexation may even have resulted, ironically, in something of an economic and cultural renaissance. One of the first acts of the first governor of the Province of Arabia, Claudius Severus, was to build the *Via Nova Traiana*, or Trajan's New Road, between 111 and 114. This was an impressive paved road that stretched for nearly 500 kilometres, linking Aqaba with Philadelphia and Bostra.

The Province of Arabia, important for its agricultural lands, cities and trade routes, had to be defended against two recurring threats from the east and south-east – the marauding Arab tribes from the desert, and the formidable kingdom of Persia. The Romans installed the Third Cyrenaica legion at Bostra to provide security throughout the province, with the governor of the province also commanding the legion. A smaller detachment of troops may also have been stationed at the Roman legionary fortress at Udruh, 15 kilometres east of Petra. Despite the increased use of the direct sea route between southern Arabia and Egypt, Petra continued to function as a trading entrepôt, for it was still an important station along the north–south inland caravan routes that linked Arabia with Syria. But now it probably derived less direct revenue from the commerce that passed through its territory, having to share the income from taxation, services and entrepreneurial commerce with both Rome and the new regional power, the Kingdom of Palmyra. This new kingdom, in the eastern Syrian desert, had started to grow in importance during the 1st century AD because of its role as a trading entrepôt between Syria and the Mediterranean world, and Mesopotamia and the east.

The security provided by the 'Roman Peace', revenue from trade, and the Nabataeans' new emphasis on irrigated agriculture all combined to assure continued urban development at Petra throughout the reigns of Trajan (98–117), Hadrian (117–38), the Antonines, and Septimius Severus (193–211). The Emperor Hadrian visited Petra in 130, during his tour of the eastern provinces, and the city was known thereafter as *Petra Hadriane*. Excavations, wall lines and the siting of burials have all confirmed that while the Petra municipal boundaries contracted somewhat after the Roman annexation, the city centre was handsomely redeveloped with a strong Roman character. New projects included, among others, rebuilding the main theatre and refurbishing the colonnaded street that probably had been first laid out in the early 1st century AD under Aretas IV. While the Nabataeans took on a mandatory Greco–Roman veneer, using Latin and Greek and even adopting Hellenised names, the enduring Nabataean Arab identity continued to make itself felt in Nabataean customs, architecture, script and even religion. Nabataean inscriptions on both the Saudi Arabian and Egyptian coasts of the Red Sea show that Nabataean traders were still active in northern Arabia, the Sinai and Egypt several hundred years after the Roman annexation of their capital and heartland.

During the 3rd century AD, Petra suffered from the regional and international political turmoil that rocked the rest of the Roman East. The Persian Sassanians attacked the province of Syria from the east and captured Antioch in 260, taking prisoner the Emperor Valerian. The now powerful Arab Kingdom of Palmyra came to Rome's help and repulsed the Sassanian invasion, carving out for itself the role of Rome's ally and protector of its frontier interests in the east, much the same role as the Nabataeans had played for Rome several hundred years earlier in the south. The Emperor Diocletian, faced with security concerns on both the Arab and Persian fronts, briefly checked the slide of the Roman provinces of Syria and Arabia at the end of the 3rd century. He accomplished this through political reorganisation, enlarging the army, improving frontier defences, reforming the economic system, and rearranging and fortifying the provinces. The northern half of the Province of Arabia retained its old name. Its southern parts, including Petra and the lands south of the Wadi Hasa, left the Arabian province and became part of the Province of Palestine, to be known as *Palestina Tertia*.

THE BYZANTINE ERA

Petra, the Nabataeans and the rest of the Roman east were soon to be overrun by the new power of Christianity, which had steadily gained ground during the early years of the 4th century. After the abdication of Diocletian, the Emperor Constantine assumed power in 312, and soon established the new capital of the Eastern Roman Empire at the site of the former Greek colony of Byzantium. In 324, Christianity was proclaimed as the official religion of the Empire, and Constantine formally dedicated his new capital of Constantinople, or New Rome (the modern Istanbul), on 11 May 330.

For the next 300 years, Petra and the land of the Nabataeans lived in the realm of the Christian Byzantine Empire. But the impact of Christianity at Petra was rather slow to arrive, and its inhabitants continued to adhere to elements of their former Nabataean cults for many decades after the advent of Byzantium.

The Byzantine period was one of steady population growth

and urbanism throughout Jordan. Petra remained an active, though perhaps not glorious, city throughout the Byzantine era. That Christianity did finally take hold here is clear from literary references to bishops from Petra, and from the symbols of Christianity at Petra itself, such as the many inscribed crosses and the transformation of the Urn Tomb into a church some time before 447. The historical references to bishops from Petra show that organised worship took place here during the 4th, 5th and 6th centuries. The last such reference to a bishop at Petra is to the late 6th-century Bishop Athenogenus, a nephew of the Emperor Maurice (582–602).

Coin evidence from Diana Kirkbride's excavations around the colonnaded street shows that a series of shops was in use here during the 4th century, while Peter Parr concludes from his excavations along the same street that commercial activity here had largely ceased by the 5th century. The excavations tend to confirm a 4th-century Syriac letter attributed to Bishop Cyril of Jerusalem that provides literary evidence of major earthquake destruction at Petra on 19 May 363. Some parts of the city continued in use afterwards, but the city as a whole probably lacked any major civic buildings.

During the 5th and 6th centuries, as Dr Tom Parker's work shows, most of the forts that formed the Roman–Byzantine security belt to the east of Jordan's cities were abandoned. The combination of weakened security and economic decline once again made Jordan ripe for conquest by more dynamic forces from abroad. In 614 Persian invaders harrassed the area during the reign of the Emperor Heraclius; the Byzantine Empire's hold on the land of Jordan had become precarious.

THE ISLAMIC ERA

The next major challenge came from the south in 629, when the armies of Islam came out of Arabia and clashed with the forces of Byzantium at Mu'tah, in south Jordan. They were initially repulsed, but attacked again and finally defeated the Byzantines at the Battle of Yarmouk, in north Jordan, in August 636. The Islamic generals marched on to Damascus, and established the Umayyad Caliphate in 661. There is some historical evidence to indicate that the Nabataeans continued trading with the cities of northern Arabia just before the advent of Islam in the early 7th century, and may have sided with the Islamic forces when the great confrontation with Byzantium finally materialised. Dr Salah K. Hamarneh of the University of Jordan suggests the remnants of the Nabataeans who still lived in southern Jordan so resented the Roman–Byzantine dominance of their former kingdom and capital city Petra that they allied themselves with the new Islamic power and viewed the surging Arabians from the peninsula as their 'liberators'. There are Arab historical references to a 7th/8th-century Nabataean *souq*, or market, at the Arabian town of Yathrib (Medina), and to an incident in the early 7th century when Nabataeans warned the young Islamic power of a Byzantine army being amassed in Syria to attack it. By this time, though, the 'Nabataeans' mentioned in the Arabic sources were most probably Aramaic-speaking peasants who may or may not have descended from the Nabataean Arabs of half a millennium earlier.

With the establishment of the Umayyad Caliphate in Damascus in the mid-7th century, the people of Jordan found themselves under new leadership yet again. But for Petra, the end had finally come. Whatever organised urban life continued at Petra was successively obliterated by a series of earthquakes during the 7th and 8th centuries. The final blow to life within the city was probably the great earthquake of 747 which destroyed so many other cities in Palestine and Jordan. The picture of south Jordan in the Umayyad era appears somewhat dim, with no significant city-remains having been discovered to date. In the mid-8th century, when power shifted to Baghdad with the establishment of the Abbasid Caliphate in 750, the entire land of Jordan declined gradually into a relatively neglected, sparsely populated district that was regionally insignificant in terms of agriculture, industry, trade, demographic power or military security.

After the early Islamic era, Petra virtually disappears from the historical record. In the Crusader period, it regained momentarily some importance as a strategic outpost, reaping some commercial rewards for the invading Crusaders. After the First Crusade in 1097–9, the Crusaders established four Latin kingdoms in Edessa, Antioch, Tripoli and Jerusalem. But it was only under Baldwin I of the Kingdom of Jerusalem that they expanded into the land east of the Dead Sea, seeking both to secure militarily their south-east flank and to collect revenues from the modest trade that still passed through the area. They called the area east of the Dead Sea and the Wadi Araba the district of 'Oultre Jourdain'. By 1115/16, Baldwin's forces had built a string of fortresses along the route between Jerusalem and Aqaba (Aila), including strongholds at Shobak ('Mont Real' or 'Mons Regalis') and Petra ('La Vallee de Moise' or 'Le Vaux Moise', meaning Wadi Musa), and on an island off the coast of Aqaba called 'Ile de Graye' (known in Arabic as Jeziret Phar'oun, or 'Pharoah's Island'). The fortifications of Oultre Jourdain were strengthened after several major clashes with the Arab/Muslim forces, including the construction in 1142 of the great Crusader fortress at Kerak ('Le Krak de Moab'). The Crusader presence in south Jordan and beyond increased steadily, for in Baldwin III's charter of 31 July 1161, he lists four fiefs for Oultre Jourdain: Le Krak, Mont Real, Ahamant (Maan, or possibly even Amman) and Wadi Musa. The Crusader presence in the Middle East was significantly curtailed by 1188/9, after the Arab forces of Salaheddeen (Saladin) defeated them in 1187 at the Battle of Hittin.

At least two Crusader fortresses built at Petra can be visited today. The main one was the fortress at Al-Wu'eira, just north of the Petra Forum Hotel. A fortress on the summit of Al-Habees mountain was probably a later subsidiary look-out installation to watch over the important communications routes that passed through the Petra basin, and that could not be adquately monitored from Al-Wu'eira. Both were abandoned towards the end of the 12th century.

As Dr Fawzi Zayadine has pointed out, there are several references to Petra during the 13th century. The Christian pilgrim Thetmar refers to it in 1217, and several later Arab writers mention the former Crusader fortresses at Petra. The Arab geographer Yaqut al-Hamawi in 1225 lists castles named Al-Wu'eira and Sela, near Wadi Musa. The Egyptian Sultan Baibars passed through Petra in 1276 on his way to suppress a political revolt at Kerak. His chronicler, Ahmed Ibn 'Abd al-Wahhab al-Nuwairi, mentions the fortress of 'Al-Aswit' at Petra, though scholars still debate whether this was the fortress at Al-Wu'eira or Al-Habees. Sultan Baibars' passage through the city suggests that for the same reasons that Petra flourished in antiquity – the availability of water sources and a strategic location astride one of the few practicable land routes to Egypt – it must have remained throughout medieval times at least a significant stop on the established caravan routes. After the 13th century, the historical record on Petra, like its tombs and temples, is silent.

THE 'REDISCOVERY' OF PETRA

The Anglo-Swiss geographer and traveller John Lewis Burckhardt 'rediscovered' Petra on 22 August 1812, and recognised its ruins as those of the ancient Nabataean capital city. Among the dozens of scholars and adventurers who followed in Burckhardt's footsteps in the next century were two commanders of the British Royal Navy, the Hon. C.L. Irby and James Mangles, who spent two days at Petra in May 1818. In 1826, the French scholar Monsieur le Marquis Leon de Laborde visited Petra accompanied by the engraver Linant. The noted British artist David Roberts visited Petra in 1839, during his travels through Egypt and the Holy Land, and made a series of now famous and often remarkably accurate drawings that are collectors' items today. The great English explorer C.M. Doughty visited Petra in 1876 and, except for the Khazneh, which he called 'that most perfect of the monuments', disliked it intensely. The Czech scholar Alois Musil visited Petra in 1896, but only published his work as the second volume of his *Arabia Petraea*. He was able to take advantage of the first volume of the monumental study published in 1904 by the Germans, R.E. Brünnow and A. von Domaszewski, *Die Provincia Arabia*. They had spent ten days at Petra in March 1897 and another two weeks in March 1898, documenting and numbering over 800 monuments, which they sited on eighteen maps. Brünnow and Domaszewski were the first to classify the monuments of Petra according to style, though their classification and nomenclature have been regularly disputed and frequently revised by scholars ever since. The German Gustaf Dalman visited Petra several times between 1896 and 1907. His work was followed by H. Kohl's research on the Qasr al-Bint, and the study of the Roman city centre in 1916 by Theodor Wiegand and W. von Bachmann.

In 1923–4, the Englishman Sir Alexander Kennedy studied and photographed most of Petra's monuments and, with the help of the Royal Air Force, produced the first accurate maps of the Petra area based on an aerial survey. He published *Petra, Its History and Monuments* in 1925.

Archaeological excavations started at Petra in 1929, when George Horsfield and Agnes Conway first dug in the Katuteh area. One of the most valuable aspects of this work was a booklet entitled *Studies in the Topography and Folklore of Petra*, by Dr T. Canaan, which documented in detail the different names the local inhabitants of the Petra area used for its monuments, wadis and mountains. In 1934, the Conway Tower (then known as the Conway High Place) was cleared by the renowned American archaeologist W.F. Albright, followed in 1936 by the clearance of the Khazneh, the Urn Tomb and the Roman Soldier Tomb. Margaret Murray and J.C. Ellis of the British School of Archaeology in Egypt excavated some caves above the Wadi Abu 'Olleqa in 1937, and in 1954 the Department of Antiquities of the Jordanian government started salvage and preservation work in the city centre, under the direction of Peter Parr. The next year, the American School of Oriental Research did some surface surveys at Petra. One of the leaders of that team was Dr Philip C. Hammond, who still excavates at Petra today. Since the late 1950s, regular excavation and survey work has been undertaken at Petra by scholars from many countries, including Jordan, Great Britain, France, the United States, Germany, and Australia.

THE PEOPLE OF PETRA AND WADI MUSA

Petra is interesting not only for its ancient monuments, but also because it is still a living community. There are two major groups of people living in the Petra area today. The Bdul live within the Petra–Beidha basin, and the Liyatneh live in and around the village of Wadi Musa. The Bdul have preserved some of the lifestyle that was practised at Petra throughout antiquity – living seasonally in tents, caves, or rock-cut houses, fetching water from the springs inside Petra, cultivating cereals and some fruit trees, and herding sheep, goats and camels. The Bdul count at least ten generations of their people at Petra, and believe they came from northern Arabia several hundred years ago. From the three families that first established themselves in Petra several centuries ago, the Bdul have grown steadily to number nearly 1000 people today, many of whom live in the new village overlooking the central Petra basin, at Umm Saihun.

The village of Wadi Musa ('the Valley of Moses') has existed for hundreds of years as a small settlement of semi-nomadic villagers. The original name of Wadi Musa is 'Elji', or 'Ildjee'. The village is the home of the Liyatneh tribe, who number many thousands of people, and include among their sons and daughters scores of highly educated professionals serving throughout Jordan and the Arab World.

The name Wadi Musa derives from the legend of Moses striking a rock here and creating twelve springs of water. The most important spring, 'Ain Musa, is located alongside the main road, at the point where the roads from Shobak and Aqaba converge at the eastern entrance of the town.

PART THREE

The monuments of Petra

GROUP 1

THE BAB AS-SIQ AREA

Al-Birka

Just beyond the car park of the Petra Forum Hotel, east of the road to Beidha, are the impressive remains of a large Nabataean water reservoir. Known in Arabic as Al-Birka, or 'the pool', its walls are partly built and partly formed of natural bed-rock. There are, in

Al-Birka

fact, two interconnected pools. The southern one, measuring 32 by 18 metres, is better preserved, with its 1.8-metre-thick western wall still standing to nine courses of stone. The total capacity of the reservoir is 2525 cubic metres.

Al-Birka stored spring waters from the Wadi Musa area and directed them by gravity into the city of Petra. It is located at an altitude of 1100 metres above sea level, or 200 metres below the 'Ain Musa springs and 200 metres above the central Petra basin. From the pool, water flowed into Petra through a rock-cut water channel that went north through the Sha'b Qais wadi, across the only remaining aqueduct in Petra, around the northern limit of Al-Khubtha, southwards behind and past the Sextius Florentinus Tomb, and finally emptied into the large reservoir next to the Palace Tomb.

Two parallel water channels (one rock-cut, the other of ceramic pipes) also carried water into Petra directly from the springs around Wadi Musa village, through the Siq. The channels powered several mills *en route*. Traces of a circular stone mill still stand some 70 metres south-west of Al-Birka.

The kilns

A large complex of pottery kilns, four of which were excavated by Dr Fawzi Zayadine in 1979-81, is located about one kilometre north-east of the Petra Resthouse, between Al-Birka reservoir and the small hamlet of Zurrabeh. This seems to have been a centre for intensive pottery production over a period of several hundred years. The large amount of distinctive Nabataean pottery found on the site suggests this was once a Nabataean kiln, though the four excavated kilns date from the Roman–Byzantine period.

The main kiln to be seen today is an oval structure sunk into the ground and measuring some 2.9 by 3.3 metres, with four heavy arches holding up its dome. Its most unusual feature is the stone archway entrance to the fire-box. The archway was isolated by bricks to protect it from the intense heat. Access to the kiln was via stairs and a passageway from the north. A smaller, beehive kiln to the east once had a 1.6-metre-wide, semicircular vestibule at its entrance. To the west was another pair of interconnected, but rather small, oval-shaped kilns. North of the kilns is a series of five adjoining rooms aligned roughly in an east–west direction, which probably originally served as storage areas for the kilns. The excavations yielded a great deal of Nabataean, Roman and Byzantine pottery, but with an obvious drop in quality over time. Dr Zayadine suggests that the need to employ mass-production techniques in the Roman–Byzantine era, in order to meet rising commercial demand, is to blame for the lower quality of the later pottery.

Al-Khan

An early 20th-century visitor's first sight of Petra would have been an impressive tomb facade in the rocks where the Resthouse now stands. It was incorporated into the Resthouse, and now forms the lounge/bar area. As you enter the Resthouse, straight ahead of you is the tomb facade. A spacious courtyard in front of the facade, measuring some 15 by 10 metres, is flanked by pairs of free-standing round columns, which are in turn flanked by half-square corner pilasters. Pass through the doorway of the tomb and enter the main chamber, now serving rather irreverently as a lounge/bar. Three large burial chambers are cut into the back wall, and four other chambers in the left wall now house dining tables. The tomb has always been known as Al-Khan, which means a caravanserai in Arabic. This may reflect the ancient use of the spacious area east of the tomb (near Al-Birka reservoir) as a camping ground for the camel caravans that called at Petra.

The rocks directly in front of the rooms of the Resthouse are also worth a quick visit. There are many single tombs cut into the tops of the rocks between the Resthouse and the car park in front of the Visitors' Centre, including a shaft tomb leading down into a chamber with several graves. Just west of the gravelled path that leads from the car park to the Petra Forum Hotel, weathered carved steps lead up to a peculiar installation that has the look of a miniature high place, complete with altar, benches, water tank and channels. Below it, towards the car park, is an east-facing tomb facade with a small courtyard in front that is reached via a carved passageway from the east.

The Bab as-Siq

The area between the Resthouse and the Siq is called Bab as-Siq (Arabic for 'gateway/door of the Siq'). Just after the steel gate near the ticket booth, to the right is the rock-cut water channel that brought water into central Petra from the Wadi Musa springs. After the horse station, the path takes a small right turn and then straightens out for about 150 metres. When it makes another gentle right turn, and heads towards the three Djin blocks, notice to your left, across the wadi, the large rounded rock with a one-metre-high obelisk carved into its front, next to a simple doorway.

The Djin blocks

The three large, tower-like carved stone structures after the bend are known as Djin blocks, or *sahrij* in Arabic. The word *sahrij* means an underground water channel, cistern or reservoir, and was probably first used by the Arab population of Petra to describe the blocks because they resemble large water tanks. The word *djin* is Arabic for spirits, phantoms or ghosts. Brünnow and Domaszewski counted 26 of these four-sided Djin blocks throughout Petra. About half are solid, while the other half have hollowed interiors that are thought to have been burial chambers. Most range between five and nine metres high, and are either unadorned or lightly decorated with simple bases, crow-step friezes, engaged pilasters, and deep horizontal grooves in the upper sections that may have had more decorative stones

The Djin blocks

inserted in them. Some have graves carved on top, while others had both graves on top and carved internal chambers. The solid blocks, as some of the early scholars who visited Petra suggested, may have been symbols of the Nabataean god Dushara, representing either the god himself or the altar used to worship him.

The first Djin block is a plain structure with no unusual features. The middle block is the smallest of the three and has a cap-like top, a cavity cut out of its lower part, and two burial chambers in the floor; a water channel passes around the lower part of the platform on which it stands. Between the second and third Djin blocks, notice the remains of a small but thick dam that blocked the wadi coming into the Bab as-Siq from the north and also carried the water pipes. The third Djin block is the most interesting because of the preserved architectural treatment that is best seen on its west side. The carved pilasters are still very sharp towards the bottom, while the horizontal grooves along the top of the block held ornamental stones that protruded slightly from the facade. A water channel passes along the cliff-face behind the third block. On the other side of the Wadi Musa is a squarish stone structure that may have been an unfinished fourth block. Small and with a 'cap' on top, it closely resembles the middle of the three blocks on the north bank of the wadi.

The small north–south wadis behind the Djin blocks have some interesting monuments. The first wadi, just before the first Djin block, has a tomb at its upper (north-east) corner with eight burial chambers inside. In the middle of the east side of the wadi is a small chamber with benches on both sides, giving access to a larger interior chamber with ground burials. The third chamber at the lower end of the east side of the wadi is a deep, plastered cistern, with peculiar cuttings over the doorway that may have supported a door or a mechanism to lift water. The west side of the wadi has two *triclinia*, or funerary banqueting halls, one of which was connected by an internal door to a burial chamber with four *loculi*.

Immediately after the third Djin block, the small wadi to the north is also worth a visit. Five metres into the wadi are four niches on the wall above you and to the right, near a door leading into a simple chamber. Above the door and niches is an S-shaped water channel carved out of the rock-face. Twenty-five metres further on, to the right (east), is a weathered tomb facade that is not visible from the Wadi Musa path. If you continue north in the wadi and climb over the fluffy-looking rocks, you enter the area known as Ar-Ramla, with its serene, moonscape-like atmosphere. Notice the many simple graves cut out of the tops of the individual rocks, some accompanied by adjacent rectangular or semicircular platforms.

Back on the Wadi Musa path, walk a few more metres beyond the third Djin block. In the small wadi coming in from the north (right) are two tomb facades visible from the path. The first is an unfinished tomb, with only its single-divide crow-step completed. The second tomb further up the wadi is badly eroded, but has three burial chambers in its back wall. The right and left chambers have side slots, to carry shelf-like separations for multiple burials.

The Obelisk Tomb, the Bab as-Siq Triclinium and the Bilingual Inscription

The Double Entrance Tomb with Snake Carving
About 30 metres before the Obelisk Tomb, behind a tree on the south bank of the Wadi Musa, is a peculiar tomb with a shaft entrance from above and a lateral entrance from the west. The lateral entrance is a passageway some three metres long and about a metre wide, with two obelisks (one seems unfinished) carved into the wall to the right as you enter. The tomb has 12 graves cut into the floor. Carved in bold relief into the west wall of the tomb are two large snakes attacking an animal, and above and to the left on the same wall is a smaller carving of a person riding a horse.

The Obelisk Tomb
Just beyond the Djin blocks, to the left of the path, carved out of the small cliff-face is an apparently single, two-storey monument dominated by four obelisks at the top. But closer inspection shows that these may be two separate monuments, the Obelisk Tomb on top and the Bab as-Siq Triclinium below. The top-heavy Obelisk Tomb is defined boldly by the four plain stone obelisks, or pyramidic *stelae* above the plain doorway. Each obelisk originally measured seven metres high, and like the two obelisks

34

The Obelisk Tomb and Bab es-Siq Triclinium

at the High Place and the smaller carved pyramidic *stelae* found throughout the Petra area, they may have represented the 'spirit' of the dead. In this case, they probably represented four different dead people. In between the two middle obelisks, above the doorway, is a recessed niche with two pillars flanking a central figure. The figure is badly eroded, but its outlines are clear and it is holding in its right hand what appear to be the folds of a cloak or garment. Three steps lead up to the Obelisk Tomb's doorway, which opens into a single chamber with two burial chambers carved into each of the side walls; in the rear wall is a single chamber with a ground burial. The rear chamber is adorned with flanking pilasters surmounted by an arch.

Some scholars suggest the four obelisks and the figure in the central niche of the facade represent the spirits of the people who were buried in the five internal burial chambers. The strong Egyptian influence is somewhat contradicted by several obviously classical features, such as the doorway's architrave, the statue in the niche and the decorative treatment of the rear burial chamber. The unique Obelisk Tomb may have been carved before the *triclinium* below, but precisely when is unknown.

The Bab as-Siq Triclinium
The Bab as-Siq Triclinium is carved out of the cliff-face immediately below a natural fault in the rock, but it lines up

slightly to the right and in front of the Obelisk Tomb. Professor Malcolm Quantrill has recently suggested that it was set slightly to the right of the tomb to give it more height, and projected from the plane of the tomb to help counter the very heavy visual effect of the domineering obelisks. Its classical Nabataean design includes, from the ground up, six engaged pilasters carrying an arched pediment, surmounted by another six squat pilasters carrying a broken pediment. The central doorway leads into a single chamber measuring 6.5 by 7.5 metres, surrounded on three sides by unusually deep benches reached by small flanking staircases. The bench around the three walls of the main chamber is a typical *triclinium* arrangement.

A *triclinium* is the Latin term for a room with three benches. At Petra, these were often used to hold meals in memory of the dead, and such funerary banqueting halls are very common throughout Petra. The French scholar Dominique Tarrier has recently completed the most thorough study ever done on Petra's *triclinia*, identifying 107 facilities that included benches. She has called them, more accurately, 'installations with benches'. Of the total, 53 were proper *triclinia* with three benches, 18 were *biclinia* (with two benches facing each other), 19 were *stibadia* (usually open-air installations with U-shaped or semicircular benches), and the rest had no benches or had benches that did not fit into any of the three main categories. Only about 25 of Petra's 500 tombs have *triclinia* clearly associated with them, suggesting that *triclinia* were more often used for domestic purposes, in the manner of the contemporary Arab *madafa* or *diwan*. Madame Tarrier estimates that only about a quarter of the *triclinia* at Petra are funerary in nature.

Why the Bab as-Siq Triclinium should have been squeezed into this limited space beneath the Obelisk Tomb is an enduring puzzle. The *triclinium* is probably the later construction, though whether or not it was related to the tomb above is unclear. There are no other examples of 'stacked' monuments like this in Petra or in any other Nabataean city in Arabia. The most likely explanation, as several scholars have suggested in slightly different ways, is that it was deliberately placed in this prominent spot in the Bab as-Siq approach to Petra in order to 'announce' the presence of the many other Nabataean classical monuments inside the city proper.

The bilingual inscription

Directly opposite the Obelisk Tomb and the Bab as-Siq Triclinium, on an east-facing rock on the other side of the path and five metres above the ground, is a lengthy bilingual inscription written in Nabataean/Aramaic and in Greek. The three-line Nabataean/Aramaic inscription reads: 'This is the burial place which has been chosen by 'Abdmank, son of 'Akayus, son of Shullay, son of Utaih, for the construction of a tomb, for himself, his successors and the successors of their (successors) for ever and after: (he has had this done) while still living, in the year ... of Mank.'

The shorter two-line Greek inscription reads: 'Abdomanchos, son of Achaios, has made this (funerary) monument for himself and his children.'

It is likely that the inscription relates to the Obelisk Tomb and the Bab as-Siq Triclinium, and if so it may help determine when the tomb and *triclinium* were constructed. The 'Mank' or 'Malk' in the inscription refers to the Nabataean King Malichus. But there were two Nabataean kings with this name, living a century apart, in the middle of the 1st century BC and the middle of the 1st century AD. The Abbé Milik, who deciphered the inscription, believes it refers to King Malichus I, the former of the two. There is no firm evidence to link the inscription with the Obelisk Tomb or the Bab as-Siq Triclinium.

Al-Madras

Al-Madras, a self-contained 'suburb' of Petra, is a 15-minute hike into the hills south of the entrance to the Siq. After the Obelisk Tomb, ignore the small blue 'Al Madras' sign to the left, and follow the line of the stone wall behind the sign until it ends at a large rock with a cave cut into it, some 75 metres south (left) of the dam. Just behind this rock is the mouth of a small wadi, not much more than a crevice. Pass through or above this wadi mouth to pick up the rock-cut approach up to Al-Madras. For much of the way, you walk through a two-metre-wide carved passage-way which turns into a veritable corridor in one place. After about ten minutes, to the right, and slightly below you, is what looks like a miniature volcano sporting a cap-like top formed by the peculiar weathering of the rock, slightly below two other cone-shaped rocks. Immediately above these, from quite a distance, you should be able to see a group of four connected staircases, at the base of which is a large tree. These stairs lead up to the area of Al-Madras.

Al-Madras is made up of two separate, but related, areas. The staircases lead up to the lower (south) area, built around a grassy, U-shaped basin full of rock-cut tombs, monuments, cisterns, niches, water channels, staircases and assorted chambers. Immediately above the staircases, and partly sheltered by a rock overhang, is a complex of two pools at different levels, carved into the rock and connected by water channels. The lower pool still has the recesses that held the springers for the arches holding up its roof. Immediately below the two pools is an altar-like area that has been called a high place or 'court', but which probably was a *biclinium*. A staircase leads down into it from the pool above, and from the *biclinium* another broad staircase leads down into the large area within the basin. At the south end of the basin are several carved tombs, *triclinia* and niches, some of which still have their original decorative elements. Next to a three-metre high, semicircular niche on the west side of the basin is a staircase leading to a broad area west of Al-Madras, named Zarnuk al-Hureimiye, which leads ultimately into the Siq just before the Khazneh.

At the lower (north) end of the basin are the remains of an ancient reservoir made up of two adjacent pools. The reservoir measures 18 metres long, six metres wide and three metres deep, and was fed by four different water channels.

From the two pools near the staircases, follow a cut water channel back up towards the north for a distance of over 100 metres, to reach the second area that makes up Al-Madras. This north region is open to the sky and, with its altar arrangement, is more obviously a 'high place'. The Nabataean high places were cultic installations with altars, water basins and benches that were also used by the Edomites before them, and are often referred to in the Bible. The altar, facing west, is flanked to the north by two interconnected pools. Facing the altar from the east is a rock-face with 20 niches carved into it. Between the altar and this rock-face, a broad rock-cut S-shaped staircase on the north side leads down into an enclosed area dominated by a massive cave with a nicely cut doorway. An inscription found here mentions Dushara as being the 'God of Al-Madrasa', making this a rare instance of an ancient Nabataean place-name that has been retained in modern times. Less than 40 metres to the south of the high place are two chambers facing west, which are full of Nabataean inscriptions. The chambers are carved in a rock-face whose nothern end has five niches above a small carved pool.

At-Tunoob

The small area on the rocks facing the dam some 30 metres to the east is known as At-Tunoob. On its west side, overlooking the dam, is a single rock with 15 graves carved into it, next to a solitary niche and another dozen graves in the immediate vicinity. A rock-face on the east side of At-Tunoob sports an impressive string of 19 small niches carved into its south end. To the north of these is a *triclinium* with a clear four-line Nabataean inscription at the top of the rear wall, over a Dushara block in a niche with pilasters and a pediment. At the far north end of the same rock-face is a tomb with four large niches carved to its right (south). Inside, the tomb has an arched recess in the rear wall with two burial *loculi*, and three more *loculi* in each of the right and left walls.

The dam, Al-Muthlim tunnel and the approach road to the Siq

At the end of the Bab as-Siq area, the Wadi Musa path climbs a short dirt ramp to the top of the dam, and the start of the descent into Petra through the Siq. The existing stone and concrete dam was built in 1964, along the same lines – and for the same purpose – as the original Nabataean dam that stood here some 1800 years ago. It deflects the rushing winter waters of the Wadi Musa away from the entrance to the Siq, allowing the Siq to be used throughout the year as the main entrance to the city from the east.

Sometime during the latter part of the 1st century AD, at the height of Nabataean power, wealth and urban development, the construction of the dam at the mouth of the Siq required an extensive remodelling of the whole area around it. The Wadi Musa waters deflected off the dam face and were diverted north, re-entering the city by passing around the north end of Al-Khubtha mountain. The water passed through Al-Muthlim tunnel (88 metres long and six metres square) that was cut out of the rocks, flowed north through the Wadi Muthlim, into the Sidd al-Ma'ajin, and westwards into the Wadi Mataha, until it re-entered the Wadi Musa in the centre of the city, just behind the Nymphaeum. Thus the construction of the dam was part of an extensive remodelling of the entrance to the Siq that included the construction of the dam itself, Al-Muthlim tunnel, an elevated approach road and bridge over the Wadi Musa, and the decorative arch over the Siq, just beyond the dam. As Peter Parr has suggested, based on the mid-1st-century AD date of the funerary *stelae* which were covered by the later approach road and bridge, this project probably dates from the second half of the 1st century AD, during the reigns of the Nabataean kings Malichus II (40–70) or Rabbel II (70–106). It is also possible however that this redevelopment of the Siq entrance was one of the first projects carried out under direct Roman rule just after AD 106. There are no traces left of the ancient bridge, but just before you reach the dam you can see on your right the substantial remains of a retaining wall; this held up the elevated approach road which crossed the wadi over the bridge to enter the Siq.

The funerary stelae

Along the bottom of the rocks facing the dam, some 15 metres to the east, workers clearing the dam area in 1964 uncovered a series of funerary *stelae*, or *nefesh* in Arabic, carved in low relief on the

The funerary stelae

rock. There were two groups: a north group of six, and a few
metres to the south another group of five, with a single *stele* in
between. The most important were the six obelisk-shaped
northern *stelae* that are still visible today, but these can be difficult
to spot in the bright Petra sun.

The *stelae*, studied and published by the French scholar Abbé
Jean Starcky, were funerary monuments that commemorated the
dead, and their architectural style clearly shows the strong
influence of Egypt. The inscription on the bottom panel of the
second *stele* from the left says it was made in the memory of a
certain Petraios, the adopted son of Taimu who erected the *stele* in
the memory of his foster son. The inscription says Petraios came
from 'Raqmu' (Petra) but died and was buried at 'Garshu' (Jerash).
This is the first direct evidence we have to support the literary
references to Petra's ancient Semitic name of Reqem, or Raqmu in
Nabataean. Based on the style of the inscriptions, the Abbé
Starcky dates the *stelae* to the period AD 50–100. They also verify
that such funerary carvings, found throughout the Petra area,
were commemorative remembrances of the dead, and did not
mark the actual place of burial.

The Djin block

Just above the opening of the tunnel, and clearly visible from the
dam, stands a solitary Djin block with a band of multiple crow-
stepping along the top. It has a large internal chamber with two
graves carved into it, entered through a door in its west side.
Attached to the Djin block on the north side is a chamber with a
partly eroded roof and niches in the back and side walls. This may
have been a small *triclinium* associated with the Djin block.

The Eagle Monument

Continue north and cross over the top of Al-Muthlim tunnel;
when you reach its far end, look up to the left, into a wide wadi
stretching away towards the west. This otherwise uneventful
wadi has been dubbed 'Eagle Wadi', after the small Eagle
Monument carved into its north face. It is not difficult to spot.
From above the north mouth of the tunnel, look several hundred
metres up the wadi, about half-way along the north face; in an
area that seems to have had white paint splashed across the rock-
face you can see a solitary doorway cut into the rock. The Eagle

Monument is next to the doorway. Just to the left of the doorway, along the north face of the wadi, is a panel containing a series of three big niches and several smaller ones. The furthest to the left contains the nicely carved eagle with downturned wings, about 1.5 metres high and one metre wide, flanked by pilasters and crowned by a pediment.

GROUP 2

THE SIQ

The dam separates the Bab as-Siq area from the start of the Siq, the 1.2-kilometre-long natural fissure in the rock that was the principal entrance to Petra from the east. As you stand on the dam, notice a ledge-like cutting at the base of the rock to the left. This marks the entry into the Siq of the cut water channel that runs along its entire left (south) side. It passes behind the two boulder-like rocks that protrude from the cliff-face, just beyond the dam as you start the descent into the Siq. Both rocks have graves cut into their tops, but are not visible from ground level. The grave in the second rock has three round carved holes to the north, and a small gaming board of 49 holes forming a square that looks like a modern chess board. The water channel passes down the west side of the second rock, next to a narrow, rock-cut staircase. Twenty metres further on are the remains of the monumental arch. Many of the early travellers who visited Petra in the 19th century saw the span of the arch still in place, though their descriptions and drawings gave rather different testimony to both its architectural style and its function. The span of the arch remained in place until the end of the last century, and fell (according to the accounts of Mr Gray Hill, an early traveller to Petra) in 1896. The arch was a decorative, single-span structure that stood proudly some 20 metres above the level of the paved street. The curved springer stones of the arch still cling resolutely to the rock-face. Beneath them are the badly weathered remains of its decorated abutments, including pilasters and flanking niches that may have held statues.

Thirty metres further, to the left, is the blue 'water channel' sign. Just beyond it, as the path turns left, are the remains of large stone blocks to the left that supported the water channel and also served as the kerbstones of the paved road. As the path turns right, to the right is the first of several stretches of the original paved road to be seen in the Siq. At eye-level, just above the kerb of the road, are the intact remains of the pressure-pipe water system made of ceramic pipes that fit snugly into one another. They were buried into a ledge cut out of the rock, and covered with a combination of stone chips and mortar. You can trace the pressure-pipe system here for about ten metres, while the rock-cut water channel is clear on the other side of the Siq. The better preserved rock-cut water channel can be traced to the left for almost the entire length of the Siq. Its level varies today because the path is usually higher or lower than the original level of the paved road, due to the erosion of the bed of the Siq by water action, and its subsequent silting up.

On the left, facing the small stretch of paved road, is the first of 51 votive or commemorative niches that were carved into the walls of the Siq. This one measures about 1.5 metres square, has three god blocks in the middle, a lintel-like groove across the top, and carved steps approaching it from the right. At this point, the high cliffs start to close in above you, and the colour of the rocks becomes more reddish. After another two minutes, as the Siq opens up, a larger stretch of the paved road to the left forms a semicircle of over 30 metres, about a metre above the level of the path. On the right-hand cliff-face is an elaborate niche, with a god block in the centre, flanked by pilasters, and topped by a pediment and six protruding god blocks. Some 25 metres further on to the right are more remains of the water system, and the cut channel to the left.

After two minutes, the Siq opens up into its widest part, with the longest stretch of paved road forming a 50-metre-long semi-circle on the left. On the right is a blue 'paved road' sign. To its left, in the middle of the Siq and next to a conspicuous tree, is the most important niche-monument in the Siq. It was uncovered during clearance work in the Siq in 1977. It is a 2.47-metre-high niche facing west, carved out of the face of a free-standing sandstone block on the very edge of a wide sidewalk, above the level of the road. Along the top is a frieze decorated with

Niche monument in the Siq

triglyphs and metopes, with an architrave below. Its facade has two pilasters with Nabataean capitals, flanking two stone god blocks cut in low relief on a pedestal. These were schematic representations of Nabataean deities; the bigger block on the left has two eyes and a nose carved into its upper half, and is thought to represent the Nabataean goddess Al-'Uzza. Anthropomorphic idols of this sort are known from excavations at Petra and other Nabataean sites in Jordan and Arabia, and this one is thought to date from the first half of the 1st century AD. At both ends of the paved road behind the niche is the best preserved example of the original state of the water channel, which was covered with flat stones and sealed with mortar.

Just after the path comes out of a long S-turn beyond the paved road, look up to your right and notice a splendid niche with ten block reliefs carved in a row, the big god block in the centre flanked by six small ones to the left and three intermediate ones to the right. After another big S-turn, the cliffs suddenly close in above you, and the path narrows quickly. You come upon a long stretch of wall to the left with a row of ten different niches. The first has three god blocks. The second from the left, with flanking pilasters and a pediment, is particularly interesting because it shows the figure of a person (probably a god or goddess) standing over two lions or leopards. A five-line Greek inscription underneath with the name of Sabinus, son of Alexandros, is probably the work of the person who had the niche made. To its right is another large niche with pilasters flanking the hemispherical representation of the city in the centre, and a three-line Greek inscription underneath. The fourth and fifth niches have pilasters and identical god blocks in the middle, and both have Greek inscriptions underneath.

As the path turns right, on the lower left side of the wall, you may be able to make out what are thought to be the relief carvings of three camels in a row. They are said to be heading into the city, with outlines of their bodies, legs and necks clear to most people. They are down at the level of the path, with their lower legs buried underground. There are two more of these alleged camel reliefs just around the corner, after a series of four more plain niches in the wall above and a single niche with four god blocks lower down on the cliff-face. About 100 metres further on, on the left wall is a single niche containing three god blocks, flanked by pilasters and topped by a semicircular arch. The path opens up for nearly 150 metres, and then narrows suddenly. You turn the corner to see your unforgettable first glimpse of the Khazneh. Just at this point, however, stop for a moment and notice more remains of the pressure-pipe system on the cliff-face to the right, at eye-level. You can follow it for some 50 metres to the end of the Siq, and for a few metres along the rocks facing the Khazneh.

GROUP 3

THE KHAZNEH AND OUTER SIQ

The Khazneh

There are few experiences anywhere in the world of antiquities as visually striking as one's first view of the Khazneh, which the German scholar Gustaf Dalman in 1911 called 'the most perfect two-storied facade which has been preserved in the East from antiquity until now'. Its name in Arabic, Al-Khazneh or Khaznet

Phar'oun, means the 'Treasury' or 'Pharaoh's Treasury'. The local inhabitants of Petra believed the urn on top held the hidden treasure of the Pharaoh, and they frequently shot at it with rifles to open the urn and retrieve the treasure. This explains why the solid rock urn is so battered. For all its beauty, however, the Khazneh has provided few solid clues about its date of foundation and original function. Scholars have debated these points without agreement for nearly two centuries, and expect to do so for many more. It is generally thought to have been the tomb of a Nabataean king, though some have also called it a temple-tomb

The Khazneh

where ceremonies were held to honour a deified king who had come to be worshipped as a god.

The lack of inscriptions and excavation evidence forces scholars to try and date the Khazneh by stylistic, architectural and decorative parallels with other monuments in the Middle East and further afield. It has been dated anywhere from the 1st century BC through to the middle of the 2nd century AD. Recent scholarship has tended to pin it down as a 1st-century BC work, perhaps from the reign of the Nabataean King Aretas III, 'the Philhellene' (86–62 BC). He expanded the Nabataean realm to include southern Syria and Damascus, from where, it is argued, Petra could have assimilated both the stylistic impulses and the actual architects and craftsmen to embellish it with such a fantastic example of Middle Eastern Hellenistic architecture. Another view holds that King Aretas IV had the Khazneh built around AD 25, having invited suitably skilled personnel from Alexandria, Egypt, to introduce Hellenistic architecture into Petra on a grand and pure scale.

The argument for foreign workmen and architects creating the Khazneh is supported by the facade's many archi-tectural/decorative elements that are alien to traditional Nabataean design. These elements include the Corinthian capitals, the many complex mouldings, the extensive use of human statues and carved animals, and the temple facade of the lower order. Whatever its precise date, it was an architectural work of the purest Hellenism and influenced the planners, architects, contractors and craftsmen of Petra for many decades. The most obvious examples of subsequent monuments influ-enced by the style of the Khazneh are the Corinthian Tomb and Ad-Deir. All three show a temple facade in the lower storey, a second, superimposed storey above, an upper storey round *tholos* flanked by pavilions, and large broken pediment on top.

The facade of the Khazneh is composed of two superimposed Corinthian orders, the lower one detached from the rock to form a Hellenistic temple facade supported by six columns, the two in the centre free-standing. A decorated pediment rises above the four central columns, on top of which is an attic that carries the upper storey. The upper storey includes a central *tholos* surrounded by columns and flanked by two pavilions with broken pediments on top. Over the conical 'tent roof' of the central *tholos* is a replica of a solitary, almost free-standing Corinthian capital, in turn carrying the nearly four-metre-tall urn. Above the broken pediments are eagle *acroteria*, and behind these are what appear to be the bases of two gigantic obelisks, cut out of the rock on three sides and connecting with the roof of natural rock over the Khazneh.

The heavily decorated facade includes the elaborate 'Nabataean/Corinthian' capitals (with their complex patterns of acanthus leaves), rich entablatures and friezes, scrollwork, rosettes, and sculptured human and animal figures, including Medusae, satyrs, male equestrian figures that watch over the dead (Dioscuri), deities, dancing Amazons, victory figures, eagles, and sphinxes or lions. The goddess on the upper *tholos* has been variously seen as Tyche, Isis/Al-'Uzza, the patron deity of caravans and caravaneers She'a-alqum, or the patron deity of the city Manathu. The entire facade is some 30 metres wide and 43 metres high.

The internal plan of the Khazneh is that of a monumental tomb. Ascending the staircase between the central columns, you enter a portico, with two richly decorated (and very well preserved) doorways leading into two differently shaped side chambers. Both chambers, which once had functioning doors, may have been burial chambers, or perhaps served the clergy in some manner. Another staircase from the portico leads up to the Khazneh's 7.95-metre-high main doorway, which was equipped with double wooden doors whose jambs can still be seen on the floor. In the threshold is a round, dish-like cutting with a drain leading to a basin on the side of the staircase. Could this have carried away liquids that were poured during libation ceremonies?

The main chamber of the Khazneh is an almost perfect 12-metre cube, with framed and pedimented doorways in the side and rear walls leading into three small chambers cut slightly higher than the floor level of the main chamber. The rear chamber has a handsome entrance, and is a true square measuring 3.4 metres on a side; it may have held the sarcophagus of the important personality for whom the Khazneh was built. The side chambers are more traditional, deep *loculi*, with simply framed doorways. These may have been designed as more elaborate chambers that were never finished.

Climbing the rock-face on both sides of the facade are double rows of what have been called 'footholds'. Similar cuttings, in single or double rows, are found in other places at Petra, particularly at quarry sites. They are thought to have been footholds or handholds, or to have held the scaffolding or lifting structure used during the cutting of the facade.

Tomb 64

Opposite the Khazneh are two other tomb facades. The smaller one close to the Siq is buried under several metres of earth; the larger tomb to its north, slightly below the level of the ground, is known simply as Brünnow's Tomb number 64, and was excavated in 1979–80 by a Department of Antiquities team headed by Dr Fawzi Zayadine and Nabil Qadi.

In the rear wall of the impressive internal chamber are three *loculi* flanked respectively by four pilasters with pedestals. The *loculus* to the right had three shelves inside it, on which were found human bones. The central *loculus* had two shelves and a silver coin of Septimius Severus (AD 193–211). In front of the left-hand *loculus*, a stone pyramidal *stele* once stood in a depressed groove. There are three other *loculi* in the right wall, two in the left wall, and three graves in the ground.

Just to the left of the entrance is the ground grave near which the excavators found a standing sandstone slab carved with a four-line Nabataean inscription. This was an epitaph of a female concubine, carved on the cover slab of the grave which slotted into a groove over the entrance of the *loculus*. It seems to date from the 2nd century AD, and further indicates that the Nabataeans at Petra placed their funerary inscriptions on stone slabs or plaster inside their tombs, rather than on the external facades as was done at Medain Saleh.

Those who are sure-footed and unafraid of heights can climb onto the rocks directly over Tomb 64 for a splendid bird's-eye view of the Khazneh. Just beyond Tomb 64 are the remains of a dam that blocked the wadi coming in from the north.

The Outer Siq

As you leave the area of the Khazneh and head towards the city, you pass through a stretch of the Wadi Musa between the

Khazneh and the Theatre which Kennedy first called the 'Outer Siq'. Just as you leave the Khazneh area and start down the Outer Siq, you pass Petra's largest *triclinium*, an almost square, whitish-coloured chamber overlooking the path from the rock-face to the right. It measures 12 metres square, and has benches on three sides and two windows in the upper north-east corner.

Some 25 metres further, to the left of the path, is a mass of fallen rocks. A huge boulder that crashed down during an earthquake smashed the facade of a Nabataean monument, either a tomb or a memorial of some sort. The damaged facade is noteworthy because it may be one of the earliest examples of Nabataean architecture at Petra. It has a row of alternating roundels and lozenges across the bottom, originally flanked by two carved pilasters (one bigger than the other) with early Nabataean capitals and bases. Only the pilasters on the right-hand side remain today. The Outer Siq is rather bare here, though about ten metres above the ground on the right you can follow the ceramic water pipes buried in the cliff-face. In a few places, the Nabataeans built small stone walls to support the pipes where they could not conveniently cut a passage into the rock-face.

Tomb 67

After about 100 metres, the Outer Siq suddenly widens to the left, giving on to three large tomb facades in a row. The first, known as Tomb 67, has the common single-divide crow-step on top, with pilasters on the facade and a double cornice over the pedimented doorway. An interesting feature is an upper chamber cut out of the space between the crow-steps. Recent studies of this chamber under the direction of Peter Parr show it to be a single room, 2.8 metres square and 2.18 metres high. Its interior is totally plain except for a small niche in the left wall, which is too small to be a grave. The location of this elevated room suggests it is a burial chamber, sited to remain out of reach of people or animals who might disturb its contents. It has a particularly handsome doorway set within a classical frame. The remains of a low stone wall in front of the door are a modern intrusion. The close-up inspection of the upper facade also showed the tomb was once covered in a dull red-brown plaster, a relatively strong material composed of an artificial mixture of crushed limestone and quartz sand, with no evidence of burnt lime. This verifies that such decorative stucco, whose colouring was probably added later in the form of a thin slurry, was used on tomb facades as well as on built structures such as the Qasr al-Bint.

Across the path from Tomb 67, you can trace the water channel that was cut out of the rock. It is largely silted up, but is visible for some 20 metres along the base of the cliff-face to the right (north) of the path.

Next to Tomb 67 is a badly eroded facade (Tomb 68) with only a double row of small crow-step pyramids still visible across the top. Next to it is the relatively well preserved facade of Tomb 69. Its design is very similar to Tomb 67, but without the chamber cut into its upper part.

Tomb 70

The next monument, Brünnow's Tomb number 70, has character-istics of both Djin blocks and carved tomb facades. It juts out from the rock-face into the path, and both its north and east faces fronting on to the path have been carved into facades. The two rear faces, however, are attached to the mother rock, giving the monument its unusual look. It is in rather poor physical shape, with a dramatic crack down the entire length of its already badly weathered Nabataean classical facade. The unique aspect of this monument is the row of little crow-step pyramids across the top, above the double cornice. Unlike the standard treatment of such crow-steps, these have been carved out of, and protrude above, the very top of the rock, to take the shape of gables forming a battlement around three sides of the monument. After Tomb 70, you pass two badly weathered facades on the left, followed by a third monument – probably a Djin block – that has split in two, its north half lying at a strange angle along the left of the path. A few metres further on is another Djin block, followed by the start of the staircase leading up to the High Place of Sacrifice.

The Tomb of the 17 Graves

Just after Tomb 70, the Outer Siq opens suddenly to the right, where six tomb facades in a row seem to rise out of the ground, each higher than its southern neighbour. They end in a fine facade with a single-divide crow-step, carved out of a recess in the cliff-face. Two chunks of rock with crow-steps broken off during an earthquake now sit on the ground near the first tomb. On both sides of the first tomb, footholds rise up the cliff-face to the ceramic water pipes. Opposite Tomb 70, a rock-cut staircase also leads up to the pipes. You can follow the pipes as they pass above the first four tombs, and are then carried across the facades of the last two, carefully buried into the architraves so as not to protrude. Between the fourth and fifth tombs, the pipes are carried across a small gap on a simple bridge of stones.

The last of these six tombs is Brünnow's Tomb number 825, sometimes also known as the Tomb of the 17 Graves. It is entered after ascending a cut staircase of six steps, which leads into a single internal chamber. Arranged facing different directions are 14 graves cut into the floor, with three more in a large rectangular recess in the back wall topped by a semicircular arch. The four corners of this recess are adorned with corner pilasters. Towards the front of the left wall of the main chamber are five differently shaped obelisks carved into the wall, with Nabataean inscriptions underneath the two biggest on the far left and right. One inscription translates: 'Nefesh of Zaid-Qawmo, son of Yaqum', but gives no clue as to when he or his offspring lived and died. The word *nefesh* in Nabataean and other Semitic languages means 'soul' or 'person'. (In modern Arabic, the word is *nefs* or *nifs*, retaining the link with the ancient languages of the area.) The carved obelisks exhibit the three classical elements in a Nabataean funerary *stele*: the pedestal with schematic moulding, the pyramid, and the terminal rosette on top. Dr Fawzi Zayadine suggests the Nabataeans' use of the funerary *nefesh* was adopted from Hellenistic customs at Alexandria, with which Petra had considerable trading and cultural contacts.

As you leave the Tomb of the 17 Graves, notice the small cleared space facing it, with two benches (a *biclinium*?) along the sides. At the point where the cliff above the *biclinium* meets up again with the Outer Siq path, a large Djin block is still attached to the mother rock to the north. It was decorated simply, but required masonry blocks to complete its upper right (south-east) corner. Notice how the ceramic water pipes were carried around the three faces of the Djin block, at the bottom of the line of pyramidal crow-steps. At the very top are three crow-step pyramids that rise above the top of the monument and seem to have been made of individual stones resting on the roof. The effect of a full line of such stones would have been similar to the 'battlements' at the top of Tomb 70.

The Streets of Facades

About 100 metres before the Theatre, the cliffs to your left (west) sport an extraordinary mass of tomb facades on several levels. There are, in fact, 44 tombs arranged into four 'streets', known as the Streets of Facades, along with scores of single graves cut into the tops of rocks. This collection of tombs appears to contain some of the earliest facades at Petra, and shows the evolution of tomb designs and decoration during the early centuries of Nabataean development. Students of ancient art and architecture should beware, however, that the changing tomb styles do not always reflect a clear chronological development, for some of the more ornate facades could be, in fact, earlier than the relatively simple ones.

Some of the simplest facades have only a single, lintel-like horizontal groove over the doorway; these seem to have evolved into larger facades with simple pediments over the grooved lintels. This arrangement may have evolved again into facades with single or double rows of small pyramidal crow-steps along the top. The bottom street of tombs shows simple facades with plain doors and two rows of pyramidal crow-steps, which later

The Theatre and the Streets of Facades

were embellished with a grooved lintel over the door, and evolved again to include two grooved lintels and a pediment over the door. The next higher street has tombs with a horizontal lintel over the door, but projecting out in relief rather than grooved into the rock-face. This seems to have evolved into facades with both a projecting lintel and a pediment over the door. To the far left is an attractive, but simple, facade; over the door is a semicircular pediment enclosing a full circle. To the far right is a larger, more classical facade with a single-divide crowstep on top. In the cliffs immediately south of the theatre are another 31 tombs arranged in two 'streets', covering a similar range of architectural styles.

The Theatre

The badly weathered Theatre we see today is what remains of a theatre that was first built by Nabataeans who were heavily influenced, or even directly assisted, by Roman architects; it was later refurbished by the Romans after they had annexed Petra in AD 106. Dr Philip Hammond of the University of Utah, who excavated the Theatre in the early 1960s, believes the Nabataeans built the first theatre on the site sometime between 4 BC and AD 27. This was during the reign of King Aretas IV, when Petra reached the height of its prosperity and 'urban consciousness'. The Theatre was slightly modified under King Malichus II sometime between AD 40 and 63 and continued in use to the end of the Nabataean period and into the Roman era. It was refurbished soon after the Roman annexation of Petra in AD 106, as part of the urban redevelopment that followed the Roman conquest. The Theatre was virtually destroyed in a single cataclysmic earthquake in 363. Its remains were re-used for other purposes during the early Byzantine period.

When it was first built, the back of the Theatre sliced through an earlier street of Nabataean tombs, taking away their facades and leaving only a row of naked interiors above the upper seats of the auditorium. The auditorium was totally carved out of the steep sandstone cliff-face, except for built-up stone stairs and a few drain covers. It was divided into three main tiers of seats, defined and separated by two lateral passageways, or *praecinctia*. From behind the top row of seats, a 15-metre-high wall rose straight up to provide the required acoustics. It also carried the upper drainage gallery, part of the elaborate drainage system to protect it from the severe erosion that would occur if the rain-water during the winter was allowed to run over the rock-cut seats and staircases. The 60-centimetre-wide drainage channel above the upper gallery and a smaller runnel above the top row of seats diverted water around the seating area and channelled it out towards the north, where it connected with the main water control system of the city. Smaller runnels, ceramic-tile drains and rock-cut canals in the orchestra and stage area served the same purpose.

The auditorium is divided laterally into six sections, or *cunei*, formed by staircases that rise directly from the orchestra floor to the uppermost seats. Dr Hammond has calculated the seating capacity of the 40-row theatre at between 6824 and 8530 spectators (allowing 40–50 centimetres for each seat). The audience entered the theatre through two rock-cut *vomitoria*, or barrel-vaulted passageways, at either end of the stage. Above the left *vomitorium* was the small, 4.2-metre-square tribunal area, with its more ornate seats reserved for officials, honoured guests, or sponsors of the performances that took place.

The 25-metre-wide, semicircular orchestra was cut out of the bed-rock, levelled, and covered with a thick layer of very hard cement-plaster. The 6.3-metre-deep stage area was partly cut from the rock and partly built, with the stage floor resting about 1.2 metres above the orchestra. Two 1.5-metre-wide staircases originally connected both ends of the stage with the orchestra, and two other smaller staircases were subsequently built between the original two, for the same purpose. The stage was once paved with handsome, well polished limestone slabs, supported from beneath by a complex substructure of bed-rock piers, arches and debris infill. Behind the stage rose the high *scaena* wall, with a marble-decorated interior wall, the *scaenae frons*, facing the audience. If it followed the standard Roman practice, the *scaena* wall would have been as high as the top row of auditorium seats, or 17.6 metres above the stage level. It was 51.6 metres wide, spanning and even extending beyond the entire stage area. The two-storey *scaenae frons* would have been elaborately decorated, forming a pleasing backdrop for the action on the stage. The Theatre's plain Nabataean capitals, and a marble statue of the naked torso of Hercules – appropriately, the patron god of

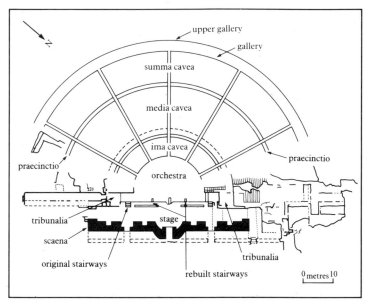

The Theatre (*after P. Hammond*)

traders and drama – are examples of the blend of Nabataean and Greco-Roman cultures that is seen so often at Petra.

Just after the Theatre, on the left (west) side of the Wadi Musa path, are the very badly weathered remains of three or four decorated Djin blocks. Facing the Theatre across the Wadi Musa path is a noteworthy group of monuments that is also very badly weathered, though the erosion of the rock-face has brought out some of the lovely natural colours of the rock. You may be able to make out here the faint traces of some columns and crow-steps of former tomb facades. Among these is a good, easily accessible, example of a Nabataean house, similar to the more famous House of Dorotheos further on in the Petra basin. This house is just above ground level, facing the north end of the Theatre, and is reached by walking over the lower rocks in front of it. It is composed of a big central chamber, flanked by several lateral rooms and a single interior room with a large, square niche in its rear wall. The room north of the central chamber leads into a smaller room to its north.

GROUP 4

THE ROYAL TOMBS

Just beyond the Theatre, the Wadi Musa path widens out into an area that is dominated today by the refreshments stand to the right known as Abu Saksouka, the name of its owner. A newly rebuilt staircase behind Abu Saksouka's leads up to the Royal Tombs, the series of large tomb facades carved out of the west face of Al-Khubtha mountain.

The Urn Tomb

The first monument you reach is the towering Urn Tomb, with its subterranean vaults. You can walk through the vaults to reach the tomb, or stay on the staircase to the right of it. The Bdul of Petra know the Urn Tomb as Al-Mahkamah, or 'the court', and the vaults beneath it are called As-Sijin, or 'the prison'. Could these names perhaps recall an ancient use for these structures in the Byzantine period?

At the last landing in the staircase before the level of the tomb, notice the original Nabataean carved steps coming down from the right. The Urn Tomb is thought to have been the tomb of a Nabataean king (the Abbé Starcky suggests Malichus II, who ruled for some 30 years and died in AD 70). The impressive exterior of the tomb is enhanced by the two cloisters at either end of the courtyard, each marked off by a colonnade of five columns and two corner pilasters carved out of the rock. The Urn Tomb's relatively simple facade is dominated by four powerful engaged pilasters, with little else in the way of ornamental work. The decoration of the architrave over the main doorway, similar to the doorway of the Roman Soldier Tomb and other monuments, reflects strong classical architectural influences, though in its overall style the Urn Tomb remains one of the best examples of pure Nabataean architecture. In the architrave, immediately above the capitals of the four columns of the facade, are the badly weathered remains of four statues of human heads. Each is set in a panel and the four are thought to represent Nabataean deities. Peter Parr noticed the evidence of deliberate defacement on the bust to the right, which may date from the iconoclastic spree

The Urn Tomb

under the Umayyad Caliph Yazid II (720–4), who ordered the defacement of all human and animal representations.

The interior of the Urn Tomb is composed of a single, nearly bare chamber measuring 18.5 metres deep by 20.5 metres wide, and some 10 metres high. The original Nabataean interior arrangement was modified when the Christian Byzantine inhabitants of Petra remodelled and converted the chamber into a church or cathedral, in 446/7. A Greek inscription, written in red paint within a frame near the left corner of the back wall, says the

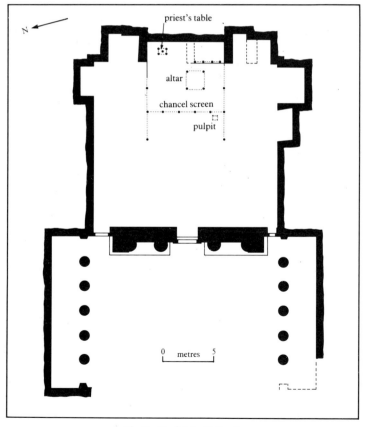

The Urn Tomb (*after N. Qusus*)

work was carried out under the authority of a Bishop Jason. You can best understand how the tomb was converted into a Christian church by following the holes drilled into the floor near the rear of the chamber. Coming out of the ends of the large central niche in the rear wall are two lines of four holes each, extending some eight metres into the centre of the chamber. At the third hole, a cross-wall of six holes marked off the chancel area, and the holes probably held up a chancel screen of some kind. Four holes forming a small square on the south side of the chancel may have held the base of a small pulpit. Roughly in the centre of the chancel area are four more holes forming a square that seems to have marked the spot of the altar. On the left side of the large chamber cut out of the rear wall are five more holes in the ground (forming a rectangle with a hole in the centre), which probably supported a table or stand of some sort. The subterranean vaults are also thought to date from the Byzantine period.

One theory has it that the interior of the Urn Tomb was in fact a *triclinium*, but its original configuration was totally erased in the Byzantine remodelling. If so, the large internal *triclinium* honoured those who were buried in the three openings high up between the columns of the facade. These were first investigated in 1962, when Mr Parr brought to Petra the skilled mountaineer Mr Joe Brown, who had made a name for himself scaling the Himalaya mountains. Mr Brown was able to climb into these hitherto inaccessible chambers, which had been thought of previously as separate entrances into a single upper chamber. His efforts have shown that these openings lead into three separate small chambers that were burial niches.

Blocking the central aperture of the three was a stone carved with the upper torso and head (now missing) of a man dressed in a toga. You can still see this stone in its original place, with classical decorative work around the opening of the burial chamber. Mr Parr thinks the person represented was probably the same person who was buried within the elevated central chamber (perhaps King Malichus II, if this was his tomb), though he also leaves open the possibility of it being the statue of a Nabataean god. The three *loculi* were placed in such an inaccesible, prominent and inviolable position, he says, to protect them from scavenging animals and men, as was done at other such elevated tomb chambers throughout Petra.

The Silk Tomb

Heading north from the Urn Tomb, along the base of Al-Khubtha, you pass two tombs with badly eroded facades showing only the bases of their columns, followed by a nicely coloured but eroding tomb facade with a single-divide crow-step on top. You then reach a facade set well back into the cliff-face, and boasting some of the most beautiful natural colouring in all of Petra. Iain Browning has called this the Silk Tomb, because 'the colour whafts so lightly across its face, reminding one strongly of watered silk...'

The Corinthian Tomb

The next facade beyond the Silk Tomb is one of the most peculiar in Petra, the so-called Corinthian Tomb. It takes its name from the early travellers' description of its columns and capitals as being of the Corinthian order, though in fact they are patterned closely after the decorative style of the Khazneh. The much maligned Corinthian Tomb has been called, among other things, a 'monstrosity', because in its apparent attempt to combine several different architectural styles it seems to have mastered none. The

The Palace Tomb (left) and Corinthian Tomb (right)

architect was obviously inspired by the Hellenistic lines of the Khazneh, which he has virtually duplicated in the projecting upper order, with its central *tholos* crowned by a broken pediment. The lower order, measuring 24.5 metres across, is a more classical Nabataean design, but is inexplicably asymmetrical. To complicate things, the doors that pierce the facade are in three different styles. The central doorway led into the left side of an internal chamber that measures just over 9 by 12 metres, and had niches in two of its walls. This large chamber is unconnected to three smaller chambers to the north, entered separately by the doors in the facade. There are no firm indications of the date of the Corinthian Tomb.

The Palace Tomb

A few metres beyond the Corinthian Tomb is the Palace Tomb, so called because it was a copy of a Roman palace design. It originally had three storeys, but much of the top storey that was built of masonry has been badly damaged and little of it remains in place. At the north end of the top storey are visible the internal arches that held up the masonry construction, which was required because the natural cliff-face was not big enough to accommodate the architect's grandiose design. The monument is thought to have been a tomb, but when and for whom it was built are not known.

The 'tomb' shows two different architectural treatments, with a broad plinth separating the doorways of the bottom storey from the two upper storeys with their many columns. The bottom storey is dominated by four doorways, divided by projecting pilasters and surmounted by pediments, with the two central doorways larger than the flanking outer pair. Above the first storey is the plinth running across the length of the facade, providing a break in the vertical design, something of an architectural pause before one ascends to the totally different style of the two top storeys. These are composed of rows of 18 engaged half-columns with projecting entablatures. The whole facade is quite badly eroded, except for some well preserved carving in the two right-hand doorways on the ground floor, where the classical Nabataean capitals are still quite crisp.

Between the columns towards the centre of the second storey is a row of six niches of different sizes and shapes. They must have been carved after the tomb was first built and used, for they do not at all fit into the overall rhythm of the columns; their careful work suggests that they were added at a time when the Palace Tomb was still in use as a funerary monument. A first-hand investigation by the mountaineer Joe Brown in 1962 showed that the third niche from the left has an enigmatic opening leading into a vertical shaft that in turn leads up to the top of the cliff, emerging behind the facade of the tomb. Peter Parr proposes that the niches, while too small to accommodate statues, may have held flat commemorative *stelae*, as did many Nabataean carved tomb facades in the Hauran (southern Syria) and Medain Saleh.

Just beyond the Palace Tomb is a cave with six burial chambers that have silted up. Some 20 metres to the north, behind a low ledge, is the large water reservoir that was fed by water channels entering Petra from the north and east. The pool measures 15 by 14 metres, with a depth of 1.5–2 metres, and was entered by a staircase cut in its south-west corner.

The Tomb of Uneishu

The most important of the less well known collection of Royal Tombs along the south side of Al-Khubtha is the Tomb of Uneishu, also known as Brünnow's Tomb number 813. It is easy to recognise from the Outer Siq–Theatre area, as it is the southernmost tomb facade on Al-Khubtha, and can be reached also by scrambling over the rocks at the end of the Outer Siq.

Excavations by Dr Fawzi Zayadine showed this to be the burial place of Uneishu, a minister in the court of Queen Shuqailat II, wife of Aretas IV. An inscription found on a grave-cover stone slab in this tomb in April 1896 by Mr Gray Hill, reads: 'Uneishu, brother of Shuqailat, son of ...' Nabataean ministers were usually called 'brothers' of their kings and queens, and Uneishu was probably a minister to Queen Shuqailat II who ruled in AD 70–6 during the minority of her son, and later King, Rabbel II. Another fragmentary inscription discovered in the tomb by Dr Zayadine in 1978 reads 'Queen of the Nabataeans'. As he points out, the Nabataeans also used the title 'queen' for their princesses. A coin find and other objects excavated here suggest this tomb was the burial place of minister Uneishu and other members of the royal dynasty for over three decades during and after the reign of King Malichus II (AD 40–70).

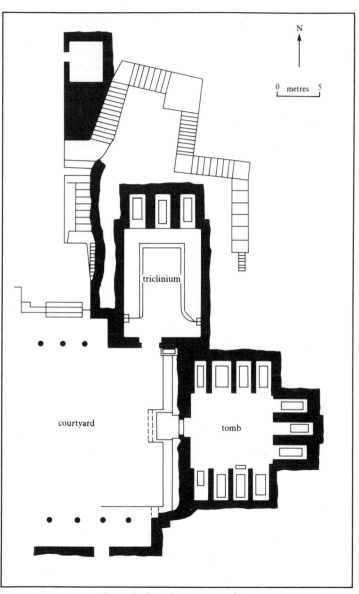

N

0 metres 5

triclinium

courtyard

tomb

The Tomb of Uneishu (*after F. Zayadine*)

The tomb facade is composed of a pedimented doorway flanked by two pairs of small pilasters, with two large corner pilasters framing the entire facade and carrying a double cornice. The top of the 20-metre-tall facade is decorated with a single-divide crow-step. The nearly square internal chamber has three *loculi* cut into the rear wall, and four in each of the side walls.

This tomb is especially interesting because it is a rare example of the complete sepulchral complex of a Nabataean royal tomb. In front of the tomb is a rectangular open-air courtyard, bounded on the north and south by porticoes of three and four columns respectively. This is best seen today on the south side, where there are clear remains of the square column bases that were fitted into the rock, surmounted by circular columns whose drums are scattered on the ground. From the south edge of the courtyard, look over the side towards the Outer Siq, to see a few metres below the remains of the lower portion of a stone obelisk that was carved out of a small platform in the rock. On the north side of the courtyard, a doorway leads into a *triclinium* measuring 9.9 by 6.9 metres, with a bench around its three sides reached by small staircases flanking the inside of the door. The *triclinium* was later used as a tomb and has three burial chambers carved into the rear wall.

From the Tomb of Uneishu, walk back towards the north, keeping first on the upper street of facades. You soon reach the only other well preserved tomb in this area, Brünnow's Tomb number 808. It also has a neatly pedimented doorway, large corner pilasters on the facade and a single-divide crow-step on the very top. Across from this tomb is a rock-cut passage some 10 metres long and three metres wide. It leads into a small, self-contained complex with a central courtyard surrounded by a tomb facade and several simple rock-cut chambers. As you walk back to the north, towards the west side of Al-Khubtha, you pass several of these complexes. There are many single graves cut into the tops of rocks, often next to small platforms. Overlooking the Theatre and the Wadi Musa path, directly opposite the Djin blocks near the Theatre, is a single grave with two cover stones still in place. About 25 metres to the south is a large carved tomb with 19 *loculi*, some of which are stacked on top of one another. Its badly eroded facade faces north.

GROUP 5

THE NORTH PETRA BASIN

The North City Walls

Just beyond the Palace Tomb, as you walk north towards the Sextius Florentinus Tomb, you pass over the buried remains of one of the two north city walls that marked the limits of the city in ancient times. Earlier writers, notably Dalman and Horsfield, showed on their maps the lines of fortified north and south city walls. Horsfield was the first to recognise two different walls in the north, which he thought were connected at Qabr Jmei'an. More accurate surveys and excavations in the mid-1960s, by a British team headed by Peter Parr, have clarified our understanding of Petra's city walls.

The wall line just north of the Palace Tomb is, in fact, the later wall, probably dating from the late Roman-Byzantine period of the 3rd and 4th centuries. The size of the city contracted slightly in this period, after the years of Nabataean wealth and civic glory had come to a slow end. While the south city wall appears to have remained in use, in the northern quarters of Petra the former Nabataean wall was abandoned and a new wall was built, slightly closer to the city-centre. The British team called these the outer (Nabataean) and inner (Roman-Byzantine) walls. The inner wall runs from near the Palace Tomb in a north-westerly direction, crosses the Wadi Mataha (perhaps with a gate through the wall just south of the wadi crossing) and rises up the hills to its highest point at the area known as Qabr Jmei'an. From here, it heads back in a south-westerly direction along the crest of the Jmei'an ridge, overlooking the Wadi Abu 'Olleqa, and down to its terminal point near the city centre. It may have terminated on the north bank of the Wadi Musa, across from the Qasr al-Bint. Or, as Mr Parr suggests is more logical, it may have turned west before reaching the Wadi Musa, and headed instead for the north bank of the Wadi Abu 'Olleqa, to protect the city from an attack down that wadi.

The original outer wall, built several centuries earlier by the Nabataeans, lies further to the north, but its route is less clear. Indeed, there is some doubt whether there was ever a continuous outer wall spanning the northern quarters of the city. If you continue walking north towards the Sextius Florentinus tomb, and then west into the Mughar an-Nasara area, you pass large sections of isolated fortifications clinging tenaciously to the hillsides. The remains of the northern fortifications are best preserved at and around the Conway Tower. There are some fine stretches of wall adjoining the tower from the south-west, and surface indications of a similar wall line running from the tower towards the south-east. While the evidence on the ground is inconclusive, it is possible that a complete outer wall did run from the Conway Tower, east across the 'Arqub al-Hisheh slopes, and across the Wadi Mataha, to join the west face of Al-Khubtha at a point just beyond the Sextius Florentinus Tomb. At the junction of the Wadi Mataha and the Wadi an-Nasara, there are impressive wall remains of a large rectangular structure over 30 metres long, matched by the standing walls of a similar and even larger stone-built structure on the south bank of the Wadi Mataha. These may have formed part of the continuous Nabataean outer wall, or, like the Conway Tower, they may have been isolated, self-contained defensive towers with adjacent walls and bastions, guarding strategic points of entry into the north side of the city.

The Tomb of Sextius Florentinus

A ten-minute walk north of the Palace Tomb, along sandy tracks hugging the west face of Al-Khubtha, is the Sextius Florentinus Tomb, named after the Roman governor of the Province of Arabia in AD 127. The Bdul of Petra know it as Qabr al-Hakim, or 'the grave of the ruler'. A now faint Latin inscription on the entablature directly above the door says the tomb was built for Sextius Florentinus by his son. Depending on how soon after the death of the governor the tomb was built, it dates from around AD 130. The inscription reads: 'To Lucius ... ninius, Son of Lucius Papirius Sextius Florentinus, Triumvir for coining gold and silver, Military Tribune of Legion I Minerva, Quaestor of the Province of Achaia, Tribune of the Plebs, Legate of Legion VIIII Hispania, Proconsul of the Province of Narbonensis, Legate of Augustus, Propraetor of the Province of Arabia, most dutiful father, in accordance with his own will.'

In the centre of the facade is a double doorway flanked by pilasters with Nabataean capitals. The doorway leads into a

The Tomb of Sextius Florentinus

chamber with a central arched burial *loculus* flanked by two others in the rear wall. When the tomb was cleared in the 1930s, it still had three fragments of alabaster pots, but everything else had been robbed in antiquity. A semicircular pediment over the doorway shows the remains of a floral design, topped by an Imperial eagle. A second tier of pilasters flanking the semicircular pediment and eagle supports the upper entablature and the crowning pediment, topped by an urn.

The House of Dorotheos, Sidd al-Ma'ajin and the Sha'b Qais route out of the city

Heading north along the Wadi Mataha after the Sextius Florentinus tomb, many people visit the nearby Mughar an-Nasara hills, before leaving Petra the same way they came in — through the Siq. For the adventurous, however, there is an alternative, but rarely used, exit route from the city that takes you around Al-Khubtha mountain and back to the Petra Forum Hotel and the Visitors' Centre. This interesting one-hour walk requires little climbing, but should only be made with a guide.

The House of Dorotheos

Much of the west face of Al-Khubtha beyond the Sextius Florentinus Tomb is riddled with caves, rooms, cisterns and niches, above which a carved channel carried water from Al-Birka reservoir to the pool near the Palace Tomb. About 15 minutes after the Sextius Florentinus Tomb, where the lower rock-face of Al-Khubtha seems to form a corner, is a group of about 20 door-and-window openings carved into the rock, with cut staircases leading up to them. This complex is known as the House of Dorotheos, and was first studied in detail by Dalman. It seems to have been the private dwelling of a wealthy citizen of Petra who may also have had some of his relatives living in the immediate vicinity.

The main feature of the House of Dorotheos is an unusually large *triclinium* with three doors and three windows. The main chamber, measuring 11.8 by 11.4 metres, is one of Petra's biggest. A wide bench goes around the three sides of the room. In the rear left corner of the bench, just above the ground, the name 'Dorotheos' is inscribed twice in Greek. This is thought to have been a domestic *triclinium* that functioned as a dining hall and/or

The House of Dorotheos

a room to receive guests, though it may also have been used as a funerary banqueting hall. To the left (north) of the house is a chamber that once served as a cistern, and a few metres to its left is a staircase that rises to two higher terraces. These upper terraces seem to have been cultic areas, for they are adorned with niches, deity blocks and altars.

The Sidd al-Ma'ajin and the Sha'b Qais route

The Mughar an-Nasara faces the House of Dorotheos from directly across the Wadi Mataha. As you walk north along the wadi, many of the lower, badly weathered Nasara tombs close in to a point where they are only a few metres away from you, on the west bank of the narrow Wadi Mataha. On the right bank of the wadi are many caves and chambers in the face of Al-Khubtha, with the water channel always above them. After five minutes of walking north, just as you cross a wall line with five courses of stone still standing, you reach the junction of the Wadi Mataha and the Wadi Sidd al-Ma'ajin coming in from the right (east). You can look into Sidd al-Ma'ajin and see that its walls are covered with nearly 100 carved niches, some with fine pilasters. This spot was obviously revered as a holy area, and suitably adorned with expressions of reverence.

The Sidd al-Ma'ajin route is usually blocked by water pools, even in summer, so you cannot enter very far. Instead, keep walking in the Wadi Mataha for a few more minutes, and climb up to an area to your right where the stone bed-rock rises to cover the ground. As you travel further to the north-east, you have successively better views of the many tomb facades on the north face of the Mughar an-Nasara ridges. After another five minutes, you enter a wide, open area. At its east end, slightly in the distance, are the impressive remains of a Roman aqueduct, still standing to eight courses of stone. The aqueduct carried the water channel from Al-Birka to the pool near the Palace Tomb. At this point you have passed around the north tip of Al-Khubtha mountain, and are heading back towards the hotel.

Keep to the right of the aqueduct to enter the Sha'b Qais wadi, now heading in a south-easterly direction. About ten minutes later, you pass along a rock-cut staircase in a 20-metre-long corridor, at the top of which a massive boulder has fallen down the mountainside, blocking the path. As you start to slide through a gap between the boulder and the rock-face, note a series of three well preserved niches in the north face of the boulder, with a big, semicircular niche below them. About ten minutes later, you cross to the east bank of the wadi and walk alongside the well preserved water channel. Three more minutes of walking bring you out of the Sha'b Qais wadi into an open area full of whitish, bulbous rocks, with the Petra Forum Hotel in the distance — almost a three-kilometre walk from the Sextius Florentinus Tomb.

The Khubtha High Places
A series of high places on top of Al-Khubtha mountain, first discovered in May 1904, have also been seen as a single complex called the Triple High Place. To make matters more complicated, there are, in fact, five separate installations that can be considered as individual places of cult or worship, so it is perhaps best simply to refer to them as the Khubtha high places. There are four different approaches to the top of Al-Khubtha: two starting from the Sextius Florentinus Tomb, a third from the steps going up to the Urn Tomb, and a fourth from the wadi north of the Khazneh.

You will need a guide to help you reach the top on all four routes, and as with all the longer trips around the Petra basin, it is most interesting to go one way and return another.

The route to the summit of Al-Khubtha from the Urn Tomb steps starts just above Abu Saksouka's refreshments stand, near the Theatre. Shortly after the start of the staircase to the Urn Tomb, turn south-east on to another ancient staircase that cuts back and forth through small wadis and gaps in the rock. The 30-minute walk to the top is a straightforward but tiring climb. When you emerge from the last small, narrow and steep wadi and reach the summit, make a sharp left turn and walk north, keeping near the west edge of the summit.

Directly above you and to the left, but not immediately visible from the path, is one of the most intriguing altars in Petra. This is a rock altar about one metre high and half a metre wide, attached to the mother rock from the west. It faces the east, and is cut out of a little sanctuary or court approached along three wide steps that lead into a gateway. The whole arrangement was

An altar at the Khubtha High Places

originally approached from the east by a 15-metre-long carved staircase, traces of which still remain.

Walk north, keeping near the west rim of the summit, and pass to the left a large, five-metre-square rock-cut chamber. Another 50 metres to the north is the first of the three high places in the immediate vicinity. It is perched dramatically on a little rock promontory, aligned exactly north–south. It has a courtyard approached from the south by a two-metre-wide cut staircase, but its unusual feature is a deeply cut semicircular cavity that some scholars have called a 'roasting oven'. To the south-west is the wide staircase that was the main processional approach to these high places from the area of the Sextius Florentinus Tomb.

Walk north and you will run into the second high place, similarly perched on a promontory, also aligned north–south, and clearly visible from the first high place. This has a central court, surrounded by a smaller, one-metre-deep square recess to the east, and an irregularly shaped chamber cut into the ground to the south-west, with a water channel flowing out of the court's south-east corner.

About 50 metres to the east is the third high place, but it is not nearly as well preserved as the other two. As you head south-east from the first two high places you run into a small dam at the top of the Wadi Khubtha, from where another path leads down to the Sextius Florentinus tomb. The dam still stands to ten courses of double stones measuring about a metre thick, with small water channels looking like spillways on both sides. Go around the dam to the water channel that fed it from the east, carved out of a small cliff-face some 25 metres further on.

East of the dam is a large open area. Look towards the north-east to a three-metre-wide passageway cut through the rocks, in whose north face is a carved obelisk about a metre high. Pass through this passageway and descend into a small, isolated north–south wadi that includes a series of niches and steps leading into the north side of the Khubtha summit. From here, about 400 metres to the north-east, is the fourth high place of Al-Khubtha. It has a deep cistern with the remains of an arch that formed part of the cistern's roof, and a nearby room that was also once roofed.

Go back to the dam to start the descent to the Sextius Florentinus tomb, either through the wadi itself or via the broad staircase west of the high places. The staircase is easier, but the route through the wadi itself is far more dramatic. In one place, the path has eroded and you have to slide down a few metres. About five minutes after you leave the dam, the path through the Wadi Khubtha becomes a rock-cut staircase, with a large water channel to the left. The water channel forks at this point, with one branch going around the side of the mountain towards the pool near the Palace Tomb, and the other branch continuing down the wadi alongside the staircase. The staircase widens to over two metres as you descend, and makes an S-turn before entering a corridor cut out of the rock, with landings in the steps and niches along the walls. The steps have eroded away just beyond this corridor, and you have to work your way down the face of the rock for a distance of about four metres, with the help of some footholds. You soon reach another impressive corridor over five metres high and ten metres long, where the steps widen out to some three metres. At the bottom of this corridor an enormous door once stood, with its doorjambs still visible. Leaving this corridor you enter an open area full of sand, with niches in the wall to your left. A yet larger staircase some four metres wide is below you, with an array of lovely colours from the natural weathering of the rock. After these steps, you can turn left to join the path that takes you back up to the Khubtha high places, or keep going straight down the wadi. A few minutes later you reach the Sextius Florentinus Tomb, to your left.

Mughar an-Nasara

The Mughar an-Nasara, like the M'eisrat mountains, is a sprawling, hilly district full of tombs and other monuments dating from many periods of Petra's life. The name Mughar an-Nasara means in Arabic 'caves of the Christians', reflecting the local tendency to equate Christian Arabs with Al-Nasrah (Nazareth), the childhood city of Jesus. Early travellers found crosses carved into many of the caves and tombs here, which has led some scholars to see this as a Christian suburb of the city.

Mughar an-Nasara lies some 500 metres outside the city proper, north of the earliest Nabataean town wall. The usual approach is a 20-minute walk north from the Sextius Florentinus Tomb, though it is more interesting, and rigorous, to enter Mughar an-Nasara from the Umm Saihun area to the north.

Another approach is to walk north for about 20 minutes through the bed of Wadi Mataha, starting from the Nymphaeum. Approaching Mughar an-Nasara from the south, you see an irregular line of facades aligned in an east–west direction along the upper reaches of the ridges that face the city. Head for the large facade facing an elevated courtyard at the highest, north-west corner of the ridges. This is a *triclinium* that is particularly interesting because of the four shields and two Medusa heads carved among the four capitals in its shallow attic storey. You can conveniently use this monument as the focal point of a visit to Mughar an-Nasara.

Stretching downhill towards the south-east are several other facades, which can be visited as you return to the city-centre. You should, however, take a few moments to visit the strange north side of the Nasara ridges. Pass a few metres west of, and below, the *triclinium* and walk north along the ancient road cut through the rocks. The road, which measures only about two or three metres wide in most places, passes a small, north-facing tomb to the left (west) as it enters the north side of Mughar an-Nasara. The road continues along the west edge of the ridge, opening on to a natural wonderland where the rock has eroded into a wild array of colours and shapes. For the next several hundred metres, as you walk north, the bed-rock seems to be drilled with thousands of small holes, and the yellow, white, red and pink rocks are criss-crossed by vivid mineral bands. The whole effect is one of a fantasy moonscape.

Just beyond the small north-facing tomb is an altar-like platform reached by steps. About 200 metres further north is a more impressive installation that may have been a proper high place. This has a very wide staircase of seven or eight high steps leading up to a platform with benches on three sides. If you keep walking north, after ten minutes you leave Mughar an-Nasara, cross the Wadi Umm Saihun, and reach the new Bdul village. There are assorted but very worn tomb facades throughout the northern reaches of Mughar an-Nasara, with a few large, well preserved facades on the highest ridges of the north face. Return along the rock-cut road to the *triclinium* with the carved faces and shields, where you can also appreciate some fine Nabataean hydraulic works (water channels and cisterns) on the platform-courtyard in front of the *triclinium*. There are about a dozen other carved facades along the cliff-face east of the *triclinium*. As you head back towards the Royal Tombs area you have a good view of the House of Dorotheos to the east.

After a few minutes of walking towards the Royal Tombs, you pass the Sextius Florentinus Tomb and enter an area of pink-coloured sand, from where you can head straight for the Royal Tombs or follow the Wadi Mataha bed directly into the city centre. The Wadi Mataha route takes you past some of the northern city walls, including an impressive stretch of the wall in the Wadi Nasara, on the west side of Mughar an-Nasara. Along both banks of the lower reaches of Wadi Mataha are considerable wall and building remains.

The Conway Tower

One of Petra's most dramatically sited monuments is the Conway Tower, at the north-west corner of the outer north city wall. It was first excavated in 1929 by George Horsfield and his wife-to-be, Agnes Conway, whose name it carries. It was investigated again in 1934 by W.F. Albright, who interpreted it as a religious high place. Thus it was known for many years as the Conway High Place; but in recent years, following its reinterpretation by Peter Parr, it has been more commonly called the Conway Tower. The Bdul of Petra call it Al-Mudawwara, or 'the rounded one'.

The Tower is perched on the summit of 'Arqub al-Hisheh, at the northernmost point of the original Nabataean city walls. It is a roughly circular structure some 25 metres in diameter along its longest axis (north-west/south-east). On the outside, it is ringed by a thick, four-metre-wide stone wall, some of whose outer stones measure over one metre long. It is best preserved on the north and west faces, where some of the original protective plastering is still visible. Inside this wall are rock-cut circular structures that looked like a 'processional way' to earlier scholars, but which Mr Parr sees as foundation trenches for walls. They surround the natural, but partly paved, rock outcropping in the centre that some scholars saw as a 'sacred rock'. From the west and south the tower abuts the main city wall, which still stands two metres high in some places.

The two-metre-thick city wall clearly served a defensive purpose. About twelve metres to the south-east are the remains of a small rectangular tower in the city wall. A similar situation exists on the south-west side of the Conway Tower, with remains in the wall of a rectangular tower that seems to have been a lookout post. Mr Parr sees the Conway Tower as part of the defensive system that protected the earliest Nabataean city at Petra. Instead of continuous walls along the north and south boundaries of the city, the Nabataeans (in this northern area of the city, at least) seem to have assimilated some standard ideas of Hellenistic military architecture, by building a series of fortified strongholds that also included associated curtain walls and smaller, secondary bastions in the form of rectangular towers. These installations would have been sited at strategic but vulnerable points, guarding the entrances to the city along the wadis from the north and south. The material evidence from the excavations, in the form of coins and pottery, indicates that the Conway Tower was in use during the centuries before and after Christ, at the height of Petra's glory as the capital of an independent Nabataean kingdom. It was abandoned as a military structure after the Roman annexation of Petra in AD 106, when, lying as it did outside the new city walls, it was used for a time as a cemetery before being abandoned for good.

The city wall leaves the Conway Tower and heads south-west towards the west side of the city centre, across the Wadi Musa from Qasr al-Bint. About 100 metres south of the Conway Tower, Mr Parr's and Dr Hammond's excavations in 1958–9 showed the city wall to be a two-metre-thick defensive structure built on bed-rock that had been cut flat to receive it. The excavations did not provide any further information on the date of the northern city fortifications, but they did turn up some well preserved Nabataean houses and ancient burials. The most peculiar burial was that of a young person in a grave made of stone slabs standing on end with a gable-like roof. Though buried with a quantity of iron jewellery, the mutilated skeleton was missing both its feet and its entire pelvis. Another burial was discovered in a large undergound chamber reached through a three-metre-deep vertical shaft.

The city wall line continues down along the ridge on the east side of the Wadi Abu 'Olleqa. About 200 metres before the wall ends near the city centre, a Nabataean cemetery known as the Turkmaniyya Graves dates mainly from the later periods of Petra's history, when the city had contracted in size.

The Turkmaniyya Tomb

This important tomb, with the longest Nabataean inscription ever found at Petra, lies in one of the city's most beautiful wadis. You reach it after a 15-minute walk or horse-ride up the Wadi Abu 'Olleqa. The two names Wadi Abu 'Olleqa and Wadi Turkmaniyya refer to the same wadi, but in practice its lower stretch near the city centre is known as Wadi Abu 'Olleqa, and after the Turkmaniyya Tomb it is called Wadi Turkmaniyya, which the Bdul pronounce Wadi Turjmaniyya.

The entire bottom half of the tomb facade has disappeared, but it once had a rather classical facade with two central pilasters and two larger corner pilasters with Nabataean capitals, all topped by a single-divide crow-step. Inside, the tomb has a 10 by 6-metre chamber, leading into a smaller inner chamber with a single burial niche in the back wall. Surviving between the two inner pilasters of the facade is the long, well preserved Nabataean inscription that has contributed immensely to our knowledge of Nabataean burial practices and tomb arrangements. It reads in full:

'This tomb and the large and small chambers inside, and the graves made as *loculi* and the courtyard in front of the tomb, and the porticoes and the dwelling places within it, and the gardens and the *triclinium*, the water cisterns, the terrace and the walls, and the remainder of the whole property which is in these places, is the consecrated and inviolable property of Dushares, the God of our Lord, and his sacred throne (?) and all the Gods (as specified) in deeds relating to consecrated things according to their contents. It is also the order of Dushares and his throne and all the Gods that, according to what is in the said writings relating to consecrated things, it shall be done and not altered. Nor shall anything of all that is housed in them be withdrawn, nor shall any man be buried in this tomb except him who has in writing a contract to be buried according to the said writings relating to consecrated things, for ever.'

This inscription provides firm evidence of the many different structures that made up a full Nabataean tomb complex. There are no remains of the other structures mentioned in the inscription, such as the *triclinium*, cistern, courtyard, porticoes, gardens, terraces, dwelling places and walls. This inscription has helped modern scholars understand the arrangement around the Roman Soldier Tomb in the Wadi Farasa, where the *triclinium*, courtyard, porticoes, reservoirs, walls and gardens are all identifiable to some extent, and can plausibly be reconstructed into an integrated complex.

Just beyond the Turkmaniyya Tomb is a similar classical tomb facade with a single-divide crow-step on top, but which has endured better the ravages of time and the elements. It has a single, low-cut chamber in the back wall with several recesses below an arched ceiling and three *loculi* cut into the right-hand wall.

Umm Saihun/An-Najr

For those who have the time and energy, an interesting half-day excursion can be made to the area of Umm Saihun and An-Najr, in the hills north-east of the Turkmaniyya Tomb. About 250 metres beyond the Turkmaniyya Tomb, walk up the Wadi Umm Saihun to your right (the north-east), heading into the area known to the Bdul as An-Njour. As you climb up the left (north) bank of Wadi Umm Saihun, you soon pass through an area of white sandstone rocks. Above you and to the left, and visible from far away, are the large, flat faces of a rock quarry at the top of the ridges. At the top of the white sandstone is the area of Umm Saihun. Across a little wadi to the north-west is the reddish quarry area of An-Najr (or An-Njour).

You can cross the wadi and walk to the summit of the An-Najr quarry, following a difficult rock-cut track to an area that may have been used for religious ceremonies in Nabataean times. Kennedy called this a 'high place' in the 1920s, based on what he saw as a series of seats cut out of the rock, near two 'triple idol blocks', or altars, each composed of three slightly convex stone blocks. There are also some niches and water channels in the vicinity, and several courtyards, all of which suggest the possible use of this area for cultic purposes.

The installations in the Umm Saihun area are rather different. There is a single, badly weathered tomb facade in the west face of the white rocks, facing An-Najr quarry. The eroded doorway of the tomb has been covered with a modern wooden door, while the only feature of the tomb that can be seen clearly is the single-divide crow-step on top. Water channels and small cisterns are found throughout the area around the tomb, and some 30 metres to the north are the remains of a small dam. On the summit of the rocks just above the tomb are several rock-cut graves and gaming boards. At the north end of the white rocks is a large cut pool, with channels leading in and out of it. About 100 metres north of the dam, in an open area overlooking the wadi, are other rock-cut installations, particularly small platforms and bench-like fixtures that may have related to the quarrying operations. A two-minute walk to the north-east brings you to the modern road to Beidha, and the Bdul village some 250 metres to the east.

The M'eisrat Mountains

The rich M'eisrat area covers the slopes and summits of two sprawling mountains north of the Forum Restaurant, overlooking the city centre and the Qasr al-Bint area. The M'eisrat mountains (singular: M'eisrah) are named after two wadis that flow into the central Petra basin from the north, the Wadi M'eisrah ash-Sharqiyyah (east) and the Wadi M'eisrah al-Gharbiyyah (west). The M'eisrat wadis and mountains are bordered on the east by the Wadi Abu 'Olleqa/Turkmaniyya, and on the west by the Wadi ad-Deir. The two mountains that form the M'eisrat district are Jabal M'eisrah ash-Sharqi (east M'eisrah mountain), between Wadi M'eisrah ash-Sharqiyyah and the Wadi Abu 'Olleqa, and Jabal M'eisrah al-Gharbeh (west M'eisrah mountain) between the two M'eisrat wadis. For convenience, they are referred to here as East and West M'eisrah mountains, and East and West M'eisrah wadis.

You can walk up into the M'eisrat mountains along any of several paths from the surrounding wadis. Perhaps the best way to visit this area is to start at the Forum Restaurant, and walk up a winding dirt path behind the restaurant to the west slopes of West M'eisrah mountain. Along the upper reaches of the west slopes of West M'eisrah mountain is a row of large, west-facing tomb facades. Just to their south is another row of smaller facades, including an unfinished tomb and two small tombs whose facades have a compressed or truncated look to them. Next to these tombs is a large *triclinium*, and south of the *triclinium*, facing a large natural courtyard, is another group of two large tombs, and three smaller ones that have been painted white by the families who lived in them. Just to the south-east of this courtyard is an isolated rock outcrop with a single tomb carved into its east face. The rippled rock on top of the tomb has been carved into a small high place, known as the M'eisrat High Place. It has an altar on top, and is approached by a worn staircase from the north.

From the M'eisrat High Place, you should be able to find the remains of a processional way that was carved out of the rock on the east flank of West M'eisrah mountain. Head for an east-facing tomb that has lost its upper part and left only a doorway flanked by four engaged columns. The processional way passes above this tomb, and goes past several other tomb facades on its route north. On the left (west) of the route is another unfinished tomb, with only its double row of crow-step pyramids completed. After a few minutes' walk up the processional way, you see in front of you a natural wall, or ledge, with a man-made wall of rocks above. This forms the south edge of a large natural courtyard with several interesting features. Carved out of the east and west rear walls of the courtyard is a series of large niche-like recesses which probably held roof beams. In front of these is an impressive plastered cistern with a staircase cut on two of its inside faces. To the west is an adjacent open courtyard, in front of a large classical Nabataean tomb facade with a single-divide crow-step on top.

From here, return to a point near the High Place where you can cross the East M'eisrah wadi to reach the west slopes of East M'eisrah mountain. There are more signs of steps and a processional way that led up to this area from Wadi Abu 'Olleqa. Just above the confluence of the East M'eisrah wadi and Wadi Abu 'Olleqa, about 100 metres north of the old school-house in the Wadi Abu 'Olleqa, there is an impressive cistern on the west bank of East M'eisrah wadi. At this point, you can see high above you to the north a tomb whose back has been carved flat to form a wide corridor at the top of the mountain. The path leading up to it over the rocks passes an interesting installation just below the tomb. This includes a tomb with a window and two *loculi*, connected by a door to a small *triclinium* to the north, which in turn leads out to an open-air platform or terrace-like area with a single grave cut into its east end. Two minutes of climbing bring you to the tomb with the flat back, separated by a broad corridor from a quarry with a Dushara block carved into its flat face.

As you return to the East M'eisrah wadi, look for a lovely little tomb cut into a ledge over the east face of the wadi bed, almost directly under the quarry. Inside, there is a semicircular cavity in the back wall with five burial *loculi*, and three ground graves in a similar cavity in the left wall. Cross the wadi and head for the nearby cistern you passed earlier. This was an important water collection point composed of three interconnected pools, formed partly by the natural bed-rock and partly by masonry walls.

GROUP 6

THE CITY CENTRE

The Small Theatre
After the Theatre and Abu Saksouka's refreshments stand, walk north along the Wadi Musa path. As the path starts a long, slow turn to the left, many tumbled stones and some wall lines appear on the left, with some large stones lying along the edge of the path. Approximately in the centre of the bend along the north bank of the wadi, Bachmann saw the remains of a small theatre, though this is virtually impossible to locate today. According to his plan, this was a Roman-style theatre with a semicircular orchestra measuring nearly 20 metres in diameter.

The Nymphaeum
The sandy path turns left and soon forks. About 75 metres after the fork are the remains of the Nymphaeum, underneath a large tree known in Arabic as Al-Butmeh, or 'the oak'. Little remains of the Nymphaeum, which was, in Roman times, a public water fountain or water collection point dedicated to the Nymphs. It was a semicircular structure, and still stands to nine courses of stone in the back, but its date of construction is unknown.

Facing it across the path is a low wall still standing five courses high, carrying the bases of two round columns. On both sides of the columns, thick walls go back into the hillside, and there is a shallow niche in the wall along the right (west) side facing the path. Bachmann called this the 'Southern Nymphaeum', but more recent scholarship sees it as a small temple or chapel of some kind. Decorative marble fragments were found here during recent clearance work.

The Markets

About 30 metres beyond the Nymphaeum, past some wall lines to the left, a wide, steep staircase leads up to the so-called Upper Market. Fragments of an inscription found near the bottom steps and the remains of two monumental plinths on the pavement indicate the staircase was entered beneath a free-standing arch dedicated to the Emperor Trajan by the city of Petra between September and December AD 114, eight years after the Roman annexation of Petra. At the top of the steps are two large pedestals that carried the now collapsed round columns. From here, you look out over a wide open area to the south and west, stretching west parallel to but above the colonnaded street. Bachmann divided this area into the Upper, Middle and Lower Markets. At the far south side of the Upper Market, the cliff-face was smoothed down to receive a stone wall built up against it, which still stands to some 20 courses.

The Colonnaded Street

Return down the staircase from the Upper Market area and continue west. Immediately after the staircase, you come upon the first paving stones of the Colonnaded Street. This street was excavated in the 1950s by several British and Jordanian teams headed respectively by G. Lankester Harding, Diana Kirkbride and Peter Parr. They cleared the full surviving length of the paved road, stretching for 240 metres east of the Arched Gate. The road is six metres wide, and is steeply arched in the centre. It is flanked by wide pavements approached by two steps on both sides, and several columns have been rebuilt along a 65-metre stretch on the south side of the street.

To the left (south) of the street are the remains of a series of poorly rebuilt rooms that are thought to be Byzantine shops from the late 4th century, most of which had paved floors. When they were in use, the formerly paved street had been covered by dirt and rubble, and the Christian Byzantine inhabitants of the city used a simple dirt road whose surface was some 40 centimetres above the level of the Roman street's paving stones. A Latin inscription on a stone built into a shop's external wall is part of a dedication to the Emperor Diocletian, from around AD 283. Evidence from inscriptions, coins, pottery and other finds suggests the Colonnaded Street achieved its present form shortly before or after the Roman annexation of AD 106.

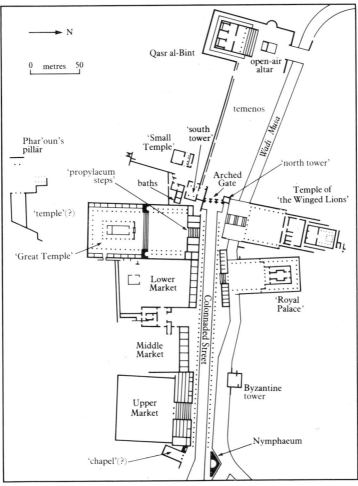

The City Centre (*after W. Bachmann and P. Parr*)

The paving stones at the east end of the street are uniformly long and well cut sandstone slabs, while those at the west end are shorter, smaller and quite varied in size and shape. The west end also lacks any evidence of a colonnade. Excavations beneath the paving stones revealed several earlier gravel-surfaced roadways and small associated buildings south of the road; these were thought to date from the earlier Nabataean city because the thick, 1.5-metre-deep foundations of the paved Roman street cut right through them. Material associated with these early Nabataean buildings included Hellenistic black-glazed pottery sherds and Phoenician coins from the 3rd century BC. It is likely that this area was part of the centre of the first Nabataean city that was defended by the early fortification wall slightly to the south, near the Katuteh and Wadi Farasa areas.

The north side of the street, adjacent to the Wadi Musa, was once lined by two-storey buildings built before the Roman occupation and the Colonnaded Street. The upper storey was entered from the street level, and was carried on arches which can still be seen in some places. The lower storey was entered from a footpath along the south bank of the wadi, connected to the upper street level by narrow, roofed staircases. A series of these rooms excavated along the north side of the street all pre-date the Roman street, and have provided such pre-Roman artefacts as 1st-century AD pottery lamps with reliefs, terracotta figures, painted bowls and some plain and painted sherds with Nabataean writing on them. The rooms between the street and the wadi were refurbished and perhaps even reconstructed, and continued in use until at least the 4th century. On the north bank of the Wadi Musa, directly opposite the rebuilt colonnade, are the standing remains of a large, unexcavated structure that has always been called the Byzantine Tower.

'The Royal Palace'

Across the street from the blue 'paved road' sign, the hillside on the north bank of the Wadi Musa is covered with the fallen stones of an unexcavated structure which Bachmann called the 'Royal Palace'. Low in the hillside along the north bank of the wadi are the substantial remains of a huge stone structure. This was part of the abutments of the bridge that spanned the wadi at this point, giving access to a courtyard in front of the 'Royal Palace'.

'The Great Temple'

About 15 metres before the Arched Gate, a large restored staircase to the left leads up into the hillside. This was the entrance to an important Nabataean public building or temple that now lies in ruins at the top of the hill. It has not been excavated and therefore little can be said about its layout, date or purpose. The staircase may be part of the *propylaeum*, or monumental entrance to a holy temple precinct. On both sides of the steps, but best visible to the left (east), are series of smaller doorways reached by two steps, piercing the south wall behind the street colonnade. These doors probably led into shops along the street-front.

The *propylaeum* steps lead up to a large open area that forms a lower terrace. Walk through this lower terrace and over some low wall lines (probably another staircase), to reach the Nabataean 'temple'. This must have been a grand and impressive structure, to judge from the large size of the fallen columns. Two column bases with several drums are still in their original place, though the upper parts of the columns have collapsed and the thin Nabataean drums are stacked on the ground just as they fell, looking very much like rows of tumbled, pancake-shaped dominoes.

Only future excavation can determine whether this was indeed a Nabataean temple. Dr Hammond hypothesises, from its size and central location, that it may have been the Forum or Agora, the focal point of the city's commercial, legal, and administrative affairs.

The Temple of the 'Winged Lions'

Ten metres before the Arched Gate the kerbstones to the right are a deep orange-red colour. Above them, a staircase at a slight angle to the street axis seems to lead up into thin air. In antiquity, this was part of the staircase that crossed the Wadi Musa on an elaborately plastered and painted bridge that led up to the Nabataean temple, on the hill above the north bank of the wadi. The temple has been excavated since 1973 by Dr Hammond. This free-standing Nabataean temple, built just before AD 27, is thought to have been dedicated to the goddess Allat or Atargatis/Al-'Uzza, on the strength of an excavated 'eye-idol' with a Nabataean inscription to 'the goddess...' Atargatis/Al-

'Uzza was the leading Syro-Palestinian fertility goddess of the day, and either she or Allat was the consort of the greatest Nabataean male deity, Dushara. Dr Hammond's latest analysis of Nabataean deities leads him to believe that the temple may in fact have been dedicated to Allat, and not to Atargatis/Al-'Uzza, though there is much scholarly debate about who was Dushara's female consort, and the deity that was worshipped at this temple.

The temple was remodelled during the reign of Malichus II (AD 40–70), when much of its original Greco-Roman-style interior iconographic painting was plastered over and replaced with solid colours. Between AD 110 and 114, the temple was partially destroyed, probably by a roof fire, and went out of use as a temple. During the next 250 years it showed some occasional casual occupation, followed by substantial domestic occupation that was brought to a sudden end by the major earthquake of 19 May 363. For the next two centuries, it was the scene of alternating phases of casual occupation and disuse, until it was again destroyed by a violent earthquake on 9 July 551. It was finally abandoned for good after the devastating earthquake of 747.

The temple is composed of a *cella* measuring 17.42 metres square, oriented north–south, and with arched supports along the

The Temple of the 'Winged Lions'

east, west and south. Its huge, 4.36-metre-wide main doorway faced the south, and probably had double folding doors. A 9.58-metre-deep entry portico in front of the main door was carried on arches. Traces of north–south double-line walls, or double colonnades, have been found heading towards the Wadi Musa for some 85 metres from the temple, with several cross walls between them. These formed part of the elaborately terraced, porticoed, colonnaded and arched approach to the temple from the Colonnaded Street.

The internal arrangement of this compact temple must have been quite colourful and moving. The four walls had alternating engaged semi-columns and niches, with ledges inside the niches to hold votive objects, such as fragments of an Egyptian funerary statuette and a Nabataean god block found near two of the

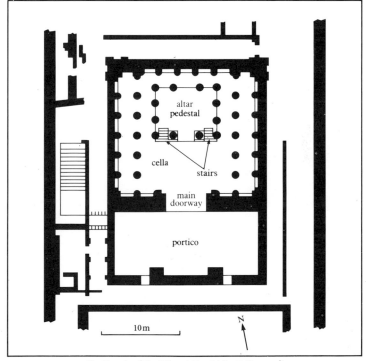

The Temple of the 'Winged Lions' (*after P. Hammond*)

ledges. (The Egyptian statuette, from Athribis in the Nile Delta, has also provided valuable proof, alongside inscriptions, of Nabataean trade contacts with Egypt.) The niches were elaborately decorated with plaster, and painted with male busts and male and female figures in classical poses, dolphins flanking a chalice, and geometric and floral motifs.

Single rows of five free-standing Nabataean columns ran parallel to the east and west walls, forming double bays on two sides of the temple. The capitals were similar to the Nabataean/Corinthian capitals on the first storey of the Khazneh. The temple also had some extraordinary capitals that were carved on two separate drum blocks. The lower was a conventional Nabataean/Corinthian style of acanthus leaves, but the upper part was a peculiar blend of flowers, pine cones, palm branches and intertwined tendrils, adorned by winged lions crouching on a bed of spreading acanthus leaves, with their wings curled down and back. At the north end of the *cella* was a raised platform, or 'altar pedestal', surrounded on each side by four columns, and reached by two small flanking staircases with gateways on the south side. A small crypt under the floor on the north side of the platform had three stone slab shelves.

Among the more interesting associated finds were a painter's, metalworker's, and marbleworker's workshops, in the complex of vaulted rooms west of the temple portico. The painter's workshop contained mixed paint-plaster, raw pigments, mixed paints and unworked pigment materials (balls of azurite and raw fibrous gypsum), all still in their original ceramic containers. There was also a pile of nineteen raw marble tile blanks that were extensively used in the decoration of the temple. The workshop and materials date from the mid-1st century AD remodelling of the temple. The marbleworker's shop, from the same period, included over 1000 pieces of marble in all stages of production, from pieces with painted guidelines to completed tiles ready for use as decorative tiles and facings. The excavators also found three marble inscription fragments – all dedicated to Aretas IV – one of which mentions a specific date in the 37th year of Aretas IV (4 August AD 26/27), and thus helps pin down the date of the original construction of the temple.

Dr Hammond and his team also excavated an area some 75 metres to the east of the temple, uncovering free-standing

Nabataean, Roman and Byzantine houses and burials, from the 1st to late 8th centuries. From some of the excavated domestic materials, including luxury imports, Dr Hammond concludes that the Roman occupation of AD 106 did not materially alter the lifestyle at Petra, and 'a relatively high standard of living persisted'. He interprets the evidence from both the burials and the houses to suggest that a 'very attenuated form of Christianity was present at Petra…and some form of the original cults of Petra appear to have continued'. Many excavated domestic objects relate very obviously to former Nabataean cults, but continued in use well into the Byzantine era. He also takes the lack of destruction evidence to suggest that 'conversion or accommodation to Islam took place with a minimum of local resistance as well'.

The Arched Gate
The Arched Gate at the end of the Colonnaded Street was excavated in 1958–9 by a British team headed by Peter Parr. It is a functional, if monumental, gate that gave access to the *temenos*, or holy precinct, surrounding the Qasr al-Bint temple. The gate was

The Arched Gate

built after the Colonnaded Street had entered service. It is not aligned exactly with the paved street, but is set at a slight angle to it. When the gate was built, the north sidewalk of the street was abruptly terminated about five metres away. The area in front of the gate was repaved with smaller stone slabs to form a miniature plaza, level with the surface of the street but two steps below the sidewalks.

For many years, the Arched Gate was thought to be contemporary with the Qasr al-Bint, given that both structures, along with the *temenos* boundary wall, were related to one another and obviously formed an integrated complex. The Qasr al-Bint was built in the period spanning the late 1st century BC and the early years of the 1st century AD. But Mr Parr and Mr G.R.H. Wright have shown that the present gate was not the original built when the temple itself was established. The existing gate is a later reconstruction that dates from at least 100 years after the Qasr al-Bint, putting it either towards the end of the 1st century AD or, as Parr and Wright suggest, even as late as the second half of the 2nd century AD. A key element in dating the gate are the four free-standing columns on its east face, an architectural feature unknown before the early 2nd century AD.

The gate was built of pink sandstone blocks bedded in mortar, with a rubble and mortar core. Patterned after the traditional Roman triumphal arch (such as Hadrian's Arch at Jerash), the gate has a large central doorway flanked by two smaller ones. The east front facing the paved street was adorned with four free-standing columns standing on square plinths, supporting characteristic zoomorphic Nabataean capitals. This blend of Nabataean and Roman architectural features suggested to Mr Wright that 'the effect of the Roman annexation, far from putting an end to Nabataean inspiration, resulted in a positive renaissance'. On the pilasters flanking the central doorway are several decorative panels with geometric and floral designs, human busts, and armed soldiers.

The Arched Gate is flanked by two large tower-like structures on the north and south, the north one in a very ruined state. The better preserved and larger south structure is more important because it may have played a role in the religious ceremonies connected with the *temenos* area. Significantly, it was entered through a large door that gave on to the south-east corner of the *temenos*. This suggests it may have been a vestibule that provided access to a series of three domed, interconnected chambers to the south, known as the 'baths'. The south building has been partly excavated, but has not been cleared enough to allow an easy visit. If you enter from the *temenos* through the doorway of the south building, you have to turn right and walk through a smaller passageway, into an area flanked by two free-standing round columns that stand out clearly from the heaps of unexcavated earth around them. They are, in turn, flanked by square corner pilasters, suggesting that this may have been a pillared hall giving access to the three domed rooms immediately to the south. You can also see the springer stones for the arches that once held up the roof of this pillared chamber.

You can reach the higher ground to the south of this pillared hall by walking up from the Colonnaded Street, about ten metres east of the Arched Gate. This route leads into an excavated room whose walls still sport the original plaster that was painted with dark red lines to resemble veined marble. You can also explore this complex of rooms from the higher ground to the south. To do this, climb the steps leading up to the Great Temple and walk west, heading directly for the blue sign reading 'the baths'. About ten metres due south of the sign, you can look down into one of the three domed chambers through the one-metre-wide round opening in the roof that permitted light to enter. Inside, but difficult to see, the room has eight half-columns built into its walls, with arched niches between them. This is the only domed room with a circular internal plan, the other two being simple, squarish structures crowned by a dome. They are noteworthy because they may be the earliest known examples of pendentives, fitting a circular, domed roof on a square room. Professor Sufwan al-Tell of the University of Jordan, who has made a preliminary study of these structures, has suggested that pendentives may have been invented at Petra.

Just south of the domed room is the opening in the ceiling of another domed chamber, but this one is blocked by stones. A few metres to the east of the first (open) domed roof, you can look down into another excavated chamber that has a square-plan staircase and more painted plaster. The plaster on the walls and the central staircase is painted red and yellow, and is best seen from the south side. The staircase, located between the three domed chambers and the lower terrace of the Great Temple, may have connected these three rooms with the higher level of the temple. This entire complex of vestibule, pillared hall, domed rooms, and monumental staircase lying south of the Arched Gate was almost certainly related to the religious ceremonies that took place in the two important temples to the east and west, the Great Temple and the Qasr al-Bint.

When the area around the Arched Gate was cleared in the mid-1950s, many decorative pieces of stonework were found and preserved. These date mostly from the period between the late 1st century and the early 3rd century AD, and their sophistication suggests further that Petra experienced something of a cultural renaissance after the Roman annexation, and may even have benefitted from the tour of the eastern provinces by the Emperor Septimius Severus in AD 199.

The Temenos

The Arched Gate was designed as a grand entrance into the *temenos*, or holy precinct, around the Qasr al-Bint temple. The *temenos* measures just over 200 metres long, but is difficult to take in all at once from the ground.

The south building of the Arched Gate forms an angle with the long south wall of the *temenos*, the principal feature of the *temenos* that Peter Parr investigated in the mid-1960s. The wall seems to have undergone repairs and some rebuilding in antiquity, and is not as homogeneous as it appears at first sight. It has several structures associated with it. The first, starting at the angle of the *temenos* south wall and the doorway into the south building of the Arched Gate, is a low platform, or dais. It is just one step off the pavement of the *temenos* and measures three metres wide and fifteen metres long. At its rear, against the *temenos* wall, is a long stone bench. Shortly after it is another 15-metre-long platform built up against the south boundary wall of the *temenos*. It is approached by three shallow, almost indistinct steps, but lacks the low back bench of the dais. Some scholars believe the alignment of these steps suggests they are the remnants of a monumental staircase that once led up to a small temple some 30 metres to the south (located on Bachmann's plans, but with no substantial structures showing above ground today). Just beyond these three steps is a water basin built into the boundary wall, beneath the visible remains of a small arch. After the water basin is another, 16.5-metre-wide staircase with only two of its bottom steps still in place. It passed through an opening in the *temenos* boundary wall that has been blocked up, though we do not know where the steps originally led.

The third main feature of the *temenos*, starting just after this staircase, is a 73-metre-long double row of benches stretching along the *temenos* boundary wall towards the Qasr al-Bint. There are two lower tiers of sandstone block benches, topped by a third row of stone blocks that form a plinth, or pedestal, carrying statues and perhaps other objects. The last seven metres of benches are structurally and architecturally different from, and more poorly built than, the remaining benches to the east. The different arrangement of the paving stones on the *temenos* floor directly in front of the east and west benches shows they belong to two different periods. It seems, therefore, that the *temenos* paving, the south boundary wall and the long run of eastern benches all date from the same period of original construction, but at some point the benches at the west end were dismantled and replaced with the existing, inferior seats.

About five metres before the benches end to the west, resting on the plinth above the seats is the remnant of a stone block that once carried a statue of the Nabataean King Aretas IV (9 BC–AD 40), according to a faint Nabataean inscription that is still visible on the block. Several other Greek and Nabataean inscriptions have been found along the upper plinth, leading some to imagine the plinth as having carried a gallery of Nabataean royal portraits or statues. The fact that the stone block was integrated into the plinth pins down the date of the *temenos* boundary wall and the west seats and plinth to the start of the 1st century AD at the latest, though they are probably slightly earlier than this. There are other Nabataean inscriptions on the upright stone blocks forming the back-rests of the upper row of benches, on the narrow fourth and sixth stones from the west end of the benches.

The benches end about 20 metres before the Qasr al-Bint, where the *temenos* boundary wall is pierced by a monumental doorway flanked by pilasters and large corner columns set on pedestals. The doorway was approached by a series of four or five steps, now badly worn. Inside the doorway are the remains of a small paved area about one metre above the level of the *temenos* floor. Where this important doorway led is also unknown. West of the doorway, the *temenos* boundary wall continues for another eight metres. Protruding into the *temenos* from this short stretch of wall is a two-metre-deep stone pedestal that still stands two metres high. Again, we do not know what purpose it served. After the pedestal, and about five metres before reaching the Qasr al-Bint, the *temenos* boundary wall makes a 90-degree turn to the south. Though it has not been fully traced from here, it is thought to have run parallel to the east, south and west sides of the Qasr al-Bint, forming a *peribolos* around these three sides of the temple. The wall emerged again just beyond the north-west corner of the temple, to join up with the semicircular recess, or *exedra*, that still stands between two large trees west of the open-air altar.

Qasr al-Bint

Qasr al-Bint, the most important Nabataean temple at Petra, was probably built during the reign of King Obodas II (30–9 BC), though some scholars prefer to place it during the reign of King Aretas IV (9 BC–AD 40). The name Qasr al-Bint is a shorter version of 'Qasr Bint Phar'oun' (Arabic for 'The Palace of Pharaoh's Daughter'). Musil said in 1907 that the name derives from a legend about a princess who lived in the temple, complained of its lack of water, and offered to marry whoever remedied the situation. One fellow said he would bring water to the temple from 'Ain Haroun 'by the power of God, men and camels', and having successfully done so finally married the princess. Dr Canaan recorded a slightly different version of this legend, which may have some basis in fact because excavations revealed the presence of a stone gutter and drain at the foot of the approach steps to the temple.

The main temple building, some 28 metres square, has squared pilasters at the four corners, and its walls still stand over 23 metres high in some places. The temple was built of local sandstone blocks set in mortar. It rests on a three-metre-high podium that protruded from beneath the temple building, and was originally surrounded by a paved court. The foundation of large stone blocks (some over two metres long) can be seen along its external south and west faces.

Worshippers approaching the temple from the open-air altar

to the north would have faced a broad, two-tiered marble staircase in front of the marble-revetted podium on which the temple rested. They entered the temple by ascending a monumental, 40-metre-wide staircase of 14 steps on to a landing or platform, and then a smaller, eight-step staircase to the level of the four free-standing and once marble-revetted columns. The 1979–81 excavations headed by Dr Fawzi Zayadine uncovered the original marble-clad steps (still visible on the west side of the staircase). In a tumble layer over the lower steps, Dr Zayadine

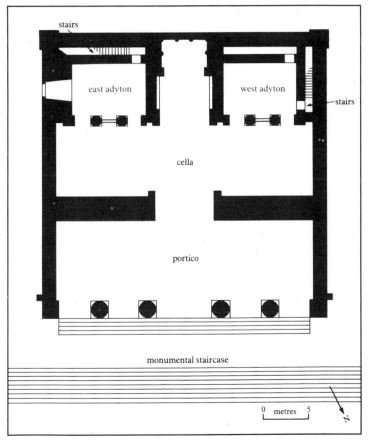

Qasr al-Bint (after G.R.H. Wright)

unearthed a Nabataean dedicatory inscription, belonging to a statue of 'Shu'udat, daughter of Maliku', probably referring to princess Shu'udat, the daughter of King Malichus II (AD 40–70).

Beyond the columns is a portico *in antis* going back into the body of the temple. The portico had a high, flat roof supported on north–south wooden beams. At the far south side of the portico, a huge door in the 2.7-metre-thick north wall of the temple gave access to the interior. The doorway once had the usual lintel across its top, with a relieving arch over it to help spread the load. Only the remains of the arch are still in place today. The doorway led into the *cella*, the main internal chamber of the temple. High windows to the left and right allowed light to fall on walls that were once covered in decorated and painted plaster, held in place with the help of the holes that now cover the walls. Along the south wall of the temple are three chambers forming the main sanctuary areas, or *adyton* in Greek.

The central chamber is the important 'Holy of Holies' that accommodated the sacred object of worship on a raised platform reached by twin flanking staircases. We do not know if the sacred object was a statue or simply a stone god block representing Dushara. But we do know of some anthropomorphic representations of Dushara (such as on coins), and it is likely that in their later days the Nabataeans adopted human representations of Dushara. If so, the main shrine to their God may have included a larger-than-life marble statue of their principal deity. The 1959 excavations of the podium area unearthed a marble fragment of a clenched human hand, from a statue that would have stood nearly seven metres high – well within the space available in the central chamber.

The back wall of this central chamber is a single wall (not double as in the two flanking chambers) and therefore required the still intact relieving arch for extra support. Was a single wall used to create more space inside, to accommodate a large statue? The two flanking chambers of the *adyton* had balcony stories above the ground floor, supported by two free-standing columns and perhaps spanned by arches. They were reached via staircases built into the double walls in the south-east and south-west corners of the temple.

Walk around the outside of the temple to appreciate its fine external decorative work. On the north-east corner pilaster of the facade, there is a single plaster panel similar to the smaller ones on the face of the Arched Gate. On the east wall, you can see the fine plaster work about a third of the way up the wall. Higher up is the Doric frieze, ornamented with alternating triglyphs and metopes. Some of the round metopes were originally ornamented with rondels, rosette medallions and bust reliefs. None of the busts remain to be seen, for at some later date in Petra's history all human representations were destroyed in a spree of iconoclasm. On the south wall, at eye level directly above the excavation trenches, are the fine remains of painted stucco that is stylistically close to the Second Period Pompeian frescoes. The scene is composed of a complex arrangement of squared pilasters carrying an entablature with pediments. In the centre of the south wall, corresponding to the area of the *adyton*, the architectural stucco depicts a shrine facade with a broken pediment. The holes which held the plaster are clear here. Similar plasterwork can be seen higher up on the east facade. On the west side, the front corner pilaster still carries three of the large square panels of decorative plaster with traces in the masonry of other panels that have fallen off. The square panels have alternating octagonal and circular designs inside the squares, an ancient motif that has been repeated in the external decoration of the modern Visitors' Centre.

The temple was destroyed and went out of use in the late Roman period, well before the earthquake of 363. Dr Zayadine has suggested that the temple may have been destroyed by the armies of Queen Zenobia of Palmyra, whose forces plundered the temple at Bostra on their march from Palmyra to Alexandria in 270. The temple was re-used in the Byzantine and medieval periods, when parts of it were remodelled to serve different functions, perhaps as living quarters, public buildings or stables. The doorway under the arch was made smaller in the Byzantine period, when the temple area seems also to have served briefly as a cemetery. In medieval days a ramp was built up to the main door, perhaps to allow animals or carts to enter the building.

The temple faces slightly to the east of north; its alignment and siting were probably determined by the natural lay of the land. The Wadi Musa to the north dictated the long, east–west alignment of the *temenos* surrounding the temple. The Qasr al-Bint was set in the south-west corner of the *temenos*, with the *temenos* wall forming a U-shaped *peribolos* around it. The open-air altar in front of the temple was an almost square structure (12 metres long by 13.5 metres wide) that still stands some three metres high. It was approached by steps from the south, and was covered with marble. Recent clearance of the area north of the altar, near the Wadi Musa, suggests the north *temenos* boundary wall returned to the south; there may also have been a northern entrance or approach to the altar and the Qasr al-Bint from across the Wadi Musa.

Why the temple itself should be oriented north–south while the *temenos* is laid out in an east–west direction is still unknown. Perhaps the Nabataean tradition of holy places aligned in a north–south direction, such as the many high places, required that their principal sanctuary to Dushara also face north. Because of the Wadi Musa, they had little choice in the layout of the *temenos*, and may have opted for an east–west *temenos* and a north-facing temple, which could have taken advantage of the natural northwards rise of the ground from the Wadi Musa to produce a stately approach to the temple. Or, as Mr Parr has pointed out, the Nabataean faithful may have shied away from an east-facing temple that would have provided the Holy of Holies with an inappropriately mundane vista over the buildings of the city centre. By facing north, however, the statue, or god block, of Dushara would have had a far more impressive view towards the mountains to the north. These included the plateau of Jabal ash-Sharra, the mountains of which Dushara ('he of Sharra') was thought to be the lord.

GROUP 7

AL-HABEES, WADI SIYYAGH, UMM AL-BIYARA AND WADI THUGRA

The Museum

The partly restored, partly original carved staircase on the east face of Al-Habees leads up to the museum and the Habees High Place. On the left as you climb are several carved chambers, some of which have been converted into storage rooms by the Department of Antiquities. Just as interesting as the small but rich collection of Nabataean and Roman artefacts is the carved chamber that houses the museum.

Earlier scholars referred to it variously as a temple, tomb or house, and its exact function is still debated. It is one of the few monuments at Petra to have a neat line of five windows above the door. The door leads into a large rectangular chamber measuring 10 by 6.5 metres, flanked by two smaller chambers. There are no signs of burial chambers inside, so this was not a tomb. It may have been the large private house of a wealthy individual, or may have related to the religious ceremonies that took place at the nearby high place, perhaps serving as a temple or an assembly point for the clergy and worshippers. Whatever its original purpose, the building now serves as Petra's museum, displaying a small but representative sample of the artefacts and decorative architecture that have been unearthed by excavations over the past half a century. Its ten glass cases are not overcrowded with objects, allowing the visitor to sample the high technological and artistic achievements of the Nabataeans without being over-whelmed by too many exhibits. The outdoor terrace in front of the museum is full of unlabelled statuary and decorative stonework. From the terrace, there is a fine view to the east, overlooking the Qasr al-Bint within its *temenos*, the Arched Gate and the Colonnaded Street beyond. This is a particularly good vantage point from which to appreciate the layout of the *temenos*, and the function of the Arched Gate as a passageway between the street and the *temenos*.

The Habees High Place

The Habees High Place is reached by an easy five-minute walk past the museum. A rock-cut route to the north turns the corner to the north-west just beyond the museum, enters a neat passageway, goes over two small staircases, passes a squarish, rock-cut water cistern to the left, and after about five minutes (during which you have commanding views down into the Wadi Siyyagh to the right) leads into a flat, open area overlooking a large table-shelf on the north-west rim of Al-Habees. The Habees High Place is not immediately visible. The first thing to look for, straight ahead and slightly to the right, is a sunken court with

The Court at the Habees High Place

several tomb facades carved into its side walls, with the single-divide crow-step of a tomb in the north-west corner of the court being the most prominent. The high place is on a rock ledge immediately behind (to the west of) the top of the prominent tomb facade with the crow-step, and is reached by walking around the south side of the sunken court.

The Court

Kennedy called this the 'garden-court', referring to the vast, flat platform to its north that was thought to be a garden. In the middle of the 'garden' platform, a solitary large rock has been carved square and adorned with a single stone god block within a niche. Steps once led up to the court from this platform, but the best preserved route down into the court is via two rock-cut staircases along its south side. Near the south-east corner of the court are many differently shaped chambers, recesses and niches. On a narrow ledge north of the court are the remains of what looks at first sight like a corridor, but which seems to have been a long, narrow water cistern. It measures some 20 metres long and two metres wide, and has a water channel spilling over its north end into the Wadi Siyyagh.

The High Place

The High Place itself is approached from the south-east on a worn staircase cut into the rock. It may have been the private high place of a wealthy family, rather than a public place of worship or ceremony. It measures just 4.9 by 3.7 metres, but has all the installations of a Nabataean high place, including a raised altar platform, benches around three sides, and an adjacent water basin. A staircase south of the High Place leads down to a lower terrace with several cut chambers with large burial *loculi* and smaller wall niches inside. There are four different staircases leading down into this small lower terrace, which also has several rectangular and semicircular basins, each about one metre long.

Wadi Siyyagh

As you start down Wadi Siyyagh, behind Al-Habees, the flanking cliffs are riddled with rock-cut chambers of many different sizes and shapes, most with their facades totally gone. Many of the chambers have small niches carved into their interior walls, sometimes in groups of up to ten niches in a single wall. About two minutes into the Wadi Siyyagh, a new staircase above and to the right (north) leads to a room which still has traces of Nabataean wall paintings on plaster. The room is locked for safety and it is not possible today to see these paintings (visitors interested in Nabataean art and painting can see the painted ceiling at Siq al-Barid, north of Petra). The Siyyagh paintings, known technically as 'architectural frescoes', depict doorways in large panels of red-brick, red-brown or ochre, framed by blue and black bands. Some of the doorways are topped by a gable with an eagle *acroterion*. The frescoes show similarities with the Second Period Pompeian illusionist style of art.

Slightly further on, an ancient staircase leads to a small sanctuary area with Nabataean inscriptions to Al-'Uzza and several carved idols.

Five minutes further on, at the junction of Wadi Siyyagh and Wadi Kharroub, the Siyyagh leads off to the right while the Kharroub goes to the left (south), to link up with Wadi Thugra. Heading right, the Wadi Siyyagh floor broadens out, and the carved rock chambers quickly cease, with only the occasional niche in the flanking cliffs. Three minutes later, as the wadi bed makes a slow bend to the left, you reach the Nabataean quarry.

The evidence of quarrying is greatest to the right (north), though on the left bank of the wadi bed there are also signs of ancient quarrying. The typical ascending lines of single and double 'footholds' are clearly visible on the north side. There are further quarrying signs ahead and to the left of the path, looking like tiered benches or seats. The narrow wadi bed then becomes sandy, and five minutes after the quarry you reach the 'Ain Siyyagh spring.

The Unfinished Tomb

North-west of Nazzal's Camp, on the east face of Al-Habees, is the Unfinished Tomb, the biggest and best known of Petra's several unfinished tombs. It shows how the Nabataeans carved

The Unfinished Tomb

their monuments from the top down, often starting at or just below a natural fault in the rock. The roughed-out Nabataean capitals and column tops indicate that this tomb would have had a facade of two engaged columns at the corners, flanking two free-standing columns in the centre. The doorway along the bottom of the facade is an unrelated later addition, as are five large niches to the lower right of the facade.

The Columbarium

Just uphill from the Unfinished Tomb on the east face of Al-Habees is the so-called Columbarium (dovecote), a repository for cremation urns carrying the ashes of the dead. The urns would have rested in the hundreds of identical carved niches in the inner and outer chambers of the Columbarium. Each niche is about 25 centimetres square, with a back wall sloping down and in, though many see the niches as being too small to hold burial urns. Scholars still debate whether this was, in fact, a final resting place for the ashes of the Nabataean/Roman dead, or, as some have suggested, a much less exciting Byzantine installation for raising pigeons and doves. Dr Hammond proposes a third theory, that this was a standard Nabataean tomb with an inner burial chamber, but was simply decorated to look like a columbarium without actually serving as one. There are five large rectangular recesses carved among the niches on the facade. About 20 metres above the Columbarium are traces of the decorative plasterwork that once covered several facades on Al-Habees.

The Columbarium

104

The Crusader Fortress on Al-Habees

A relatively easy 10-minute climb on staircases and ramps brings
you to the ruined Crusader Fortress on top of Al-Habees, from
where you have a fine view over the entire central Petra basin.

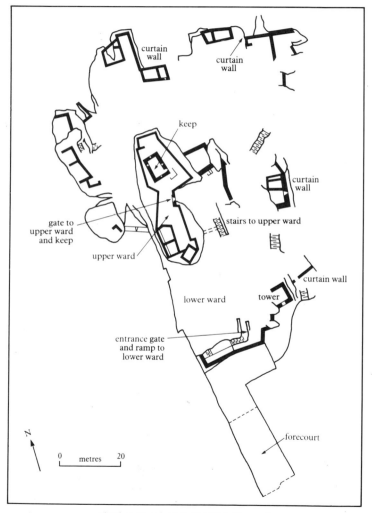

Al-Habees Crusader Fortress (*after P. Hammond*)

The main Crusader fortresses in Oultre Jourdain usually had associated with them smaller forts that acted as subsidiary lookouts. The Crusader Fortress of Al-Habees is one of these subsidiary installations, relating to the larger mother fortress at Al-Wu'eira. It was a secondary fortress, designed and sited to control the strategic communication route within the Petra basin that was not in sight of Al-Wu'eira Fortress. That it was an outpost with regularly rotated small contingents from the Wu'eira Fortress, rather than a permanent garrison designed to repulse an attack, is suggested by several factors: its small size, its diminutive keep, and the absence of structures that would have been mandatory in larger fortresses (and are, indeed, found at Wu'eira), such as storage rooms, a chapel or a 'great hall'. It may have been known to the Crusaders as the fortress of Sela or Aswit, though neither of these names have been conclusively proven to be the medieval name for the Habees Fortress. Dr Hammond, who surveyed the fortress in 1959, believes it was built after Al-Wu'eira, sometime between 1116 and 1188. Al-Habees seems to have been peacefully abandoned (there are no signs of violent destruction) towards the end of the 12th century, probably for military reasons dictated by the anticipated downfall of Al-Wu'eira.

To reach the fortress, head for the blue 'Habis Crusader Castle' sign along the south-east base of Al-Habees. From the sign, a rebuilt staircase follows the original Crusader ascent to the entrance of the fortress. Just a few minutes after the start of the staircase, you step up onto the open forecourt area, a terrace-like projection along the south side of Al-Habees. This is the lowest level of the fortress, which had four main parts to it: the keep, or observation tower, at the summit; the upper ward surrounding the keep; the lower ward; and the forecourt.

Continuing up the staircase, you pass through a doorway whose threshold still shows the semicircular grooves made by its swinging doors. After the steps, you walk over a modern wooden plank bridge, and then pass through another doorway into the lower ward area. Still in place above the door are the cut recesses that once held the springer stones for the vault over the entry ramp, which was flanked by adjacent towers or guardrooms. From the doorway into the lower ward, a 20-metre scramble up the rock-strewn ground to the north brings you to a squarish room carved out of the rock, and an arched entrance to an adjacent chamber. A staircase in front of these chambers leads up the final few metres, where you pass through a doorway into the upper ward. At the summit of the upper ward, reached by another staircase, is the keep of the castle, its main lookout point.

From the small, squarish keep, you have a commanding view of the northern and southern routes into the city. Below you to the east, the entire capital city, and most of the Qasr al-Bint, are visible. The south-east and east sides of the fortress are riddled with the remains of rooms, walls, subterranean support arches, staircases and towers, with some walls still standing to over 15 courses of stone (with a single firing slit for archers still in place). Walking north along the lower ward, you have a fine view back on to the cistern's large north wall, still standing to 38 courses of stone, with the walls of the keep directly above. A large rock-cut staircase leads down to lower levels along the east side of the fortress, from where you have a panoramic view over the city centre, the entire Qasr al-Bint, and the West Katuteh excavation some 50 metres east of Al-Habees. There are also many walls standing on the north and west sides of the fortress, often connected by staircases.

Umm al-Biyara

The massive rock of Umm al-Biyara towers over central Petra from the south-west, with the Wadi Thugra and the smaller rock of Al-Habees lying between it and the city centre. The view from the top is well worth the hard, 40-minute climb, but this trip should be made only with a local guide who knows the way up, because the path is not always clear and it can be dangerous to stray from it. Approaching Umm al-Biyara, from near Phar'oun's Pillar, you have a fine view of the varied facades along its base. These are a combination of houses and tombs, sited along natural faults in the rock that have been exploited to form four tiers, or 'streets'. The different styles of these facades, as Mrs Crystal-M. Bennett has pointed out, reflect the evolution of Nabataean architecture over a period of time. At the left (south) end of the upper row of monuments is a large tomb facade that rises higher than the others. This tomb, with two pilasters flanking the facade and the typical large single crow-step on top, has been carved well back into the cliff-face, leaving two steeply angled buttresses on both sides. Immediately to the left (south) of this tomb are two smaller tomb facades, with a large, gorge-like crevice in the rock between them. This crevice is the start of the path to the top of the mountain. Just below it is a blue sign that reads 'Umm al Biyara'.

From the sign, tumbled rocks prevent you from going straight up the opening in the rock, as the Nabataeans did, so you have to make a five-minute detour to the south, up and around a lone tree. In the south wall of a cave to the left as you reach the cliff-face is a lightly carved obelisk *nefesh* on a rectangular base. Passing three niches to the left, you reach the natural gorge in the mountain, into which the Nabataeans built an impressive staircase that marked the start of the route to the summit. Just after the first few steps you pass under the remains of an arch that spanned the staircase. This one is slightly better preserved than the arch in the Siq, and has ten courses of double stones still in place, along with the springer stones for the arch itself. A two-minute walk beyond the staircase brings you to the large double-ramp corridor. It rises first as a broad, single passageway, reaches a wide landing, and then turns back 180 degrees and splits into two flanking ramps. The southern of the two ramps is best preserved, and seems slightly narrower than its northern twin.

From here, it is a 30-minute hard climb to the summit, along the remains of carved paths and staircases. This was obviously a processional way of some sort, leading to a Nabataean temple or sanctuary that has left behind a mass of tumbled ruins along the north-east edge of the summit. After a scramble on all fours up a small, steep gully (because the adjacent carved staircase has been filled with tumbled rocks), you reach the south side of the summit. The summit slopes from west to east at a 20-degree angle. As you walk north, you come upon the trenches of the excavations that Mrs Bennett led here for three years in the mid-1960s. She uncovered the remains of Iron Age houses from the 7th century BC. These were part of a small Edomite settlement that existed some 300 years before the Nabataeans took over and developed Petra into a rich and magnificent city.

The excavations revealed a line of Edomite rooms and houses on both sides of a north–south spine wall. The room walls were built by stacking the uneven blocks of limestone that could be broken off easily along their natural horizontal striations. In some

Edomite settlement on the summit of Umm al-Biyara

places, the walls stand to a height of two metres, probably their original height. The excavated artefacts, including loom weights, much domestic pottery (storage jars, plates, bowls), shells, lamps, and a few metal objects (including just six arrowheads) suggested to Mrs Bennett that this was a small, non-military domestic settlement of perhaps 100 people. It lasted for only one or two generations during the first half of the 7th century BC, and seems to have been abandoned after a major fire. A room towards the north end of the complex had a special plastered floor built above the regular bed-rock level. This has been interpreted as a storage room for bags of the incense that was important in the trade between the Edomites and the peoples of southern Arabia. In one room, the excavators found a seal impression attached to a sack and still showing the imprints of the sack's threads.

The name Umm al-Biyara means 'mother of cisterns' in

Arabic, after the nine rock-cut, plastered cisterns and associated water channels along the north-east edge of the summit. They are thought to be Edomite cisterns, but cannot be dated conclusively and may, in fact, be Nabataean.

One of the important finds that helped date the Edomite settlement was a clay royal seal impression that was baked hard in the final fire and preserved. It was the impression of an Edomite king named Qos Gabr, twice mentioned in the annals of the 7th-century BC Assyrian kings Esarhaddon (680–669) and Assurbanipal (668–633).

One of the aims of the excavations was to determine if Umm al-Biyara was the 'Sela' mentioned several times in the Bible (2nd Chronicles 25:11–12 and 2nd Kings 14:7). The biblical tales recount the exploits of the 9th-century BC King Amaziah of Judaea, who captured 10,000 Edomites and marched them to the summit of the Edomite rock stronghold at Sela, before throwing them down to their deaths. The archaeological evidence suggests that the Edomite settlement here existed more than 100 years after the time of King Amaziah. Mrs Bennett and others feel a better candidate for the Sela of the Bible is the village near Tafileh that is still known in Arabic as Sela' or Sil'.

There is some evidence for a brief reoccupation of the site in the Hellenistic era, after the early 4th century BC. Widespread Nabataean ruins along the east rim of the summit attest to a significant Nabataean presence here. These include many wall lines, decorative stones, corner pilasters and the remains of rooms. At the east end of the summit are the foundations of a large building with an impressive east–west staircase, perched on a spot overlooking the Qasr al-Bint and the entire city centre. The typical Nabataean tooling of the stone and the Nabataean pottery found here suggest that this may have been a small Nabataean temple. Among the ruins are two large fragments of a late Nabataean frieze (showing strong Hellenistic influences) on which are the carved remains of Eros figures with floral designs in their outstretched hands.

At the north-west corner of the summit, in a now hard-to-reach and partly collapsed grotto, are the remains of what may have been a small sanctuary associated with the Nabataean temple on Umm al-Biyara. It consists of a fallen wall with some inscriptions beneath seven niche-altars and Dushara god blocks,

110

facing a rock-face with more inscriptions and graffiti. The French scholar J.T. Milik sees this as a sanctuary dedicated to the god Zeus–Dushara, reflecting the syncretism between Nabataean and Hellenistic deities that is a well attested feature of Nabataean religion.

The Snake Monument
The striking but rarely visited Snake Monument takes the form of a snake coiled three times on top of a two-metre-square pedestal. It is carved from the top of a small promontory jutting out from a

The Snake Monument

semicircular basin that overlooks the south end of the Wadi Thugra from the east bank. As you walk south in the Wadi Thugra, away from central Petra, it will come into sight in front of you and high to the left. Just beneath it is a large Djin block with a carved door. To your right is a smaller Djin block forming part of a complex that also includes carved chambers, platforms, staircases, cisterns and graves. The easiest way to find the Snake Monument is first to spot these two Djin blocks as you walk south through the Wadi Thugra.

From the wadi floor, a small processional way carved from the rock approaches the Snake Monument from the north-west. Dr Hammond notes that the lack of any cultic apparatus and the very small levelled-off area immediately around the monument preclude its use for major religious ceremonies. Because the head of the snake directly overlooks a sprawling cemetery area, Dr Hammond believes that 'it would appear more than probable that the Snake Monument served as the protector of the necropolis, probably in the broadest sense (i.e., against human intrusion – for which cultic and legal interdiction served later – and as a potent force at work for the 'health' of the dead in the after-life as well)'.

The tombs in this area, among the oldest types at Petra, and the comparatively simple workmanship of the monument's carving, both suggest it dates from an early period of Petra's development, perhaps in the 2nd or 3rd centuries BC.

GROUP 8

SABRA AND JABAL HAROON

Sabra

For the hardy and serious visitor who wants to see all the attractions of the Petra area, a day-trip to the Nabataean 'suburb' of Sabra is a must. From the centre of Petra, Sabra is a two-hour journey each way, on horseback or on foot, and you should take along some food and water. From near the Theatre, the fastest route to Sabra is along the Wadi Farasa, past Wadi Nmeir and

Wadi Umm Rattan to the east, through the broad, open farmed area called Al-Addja, past two prominent mountains to your left (east) called Ad-Dabba, and finally, after an hour of walking or riding, into the Ragbat al-Btahi area, from where you look down from higher ground into Wadi Sabra stretching away to the south. You descend into the wadi along its west bank, slowly and carefuly navigating a series of sharp hairpin turns. After about 30–40 minutes, the narrow wadi bed suddenly opens up into a lush, green expanse nearly 50 metres wide. Following the east side of the wadi bed, you come upon the remains of walls and buildings protruding from the right side of the wadi. To your left, tucked into a large crevice at the foot of the sheer cliff-face, is the theatre that is Sabra's best known monument.

The nearby perennial spring, 'Ain Sabra, was one reason for a permanent community here, though what the Nabataeans and Romans who lived here actually did is unclear. Sabra has been seen variously as a Nabataean suburb, a mining and smelting centre, a trading station, or a Roman winter resort and military outpost whose theatre was flooded with water and used for mock naval battles.

Dr Manfred Lindner of West Germany, who has studied the Sabra district extensively in recent years, provided the first detailed analysis of the theatre. His work, complemented by the fieldwork of Dr Fawzi Zayadine and the Jordanian Department of Antiquities, indicates that Sabra probably started as a Nabataean settlement during the 1st century AD, but continued to be used and developed by the Romans after they annexed Petra in AD 106.

The theatre is carved out of a sandstone rock gorge in the side of the steep Jabal al-Jathum. It is a Greek, rather than a Roman-style theatre, for the auditorium seats extend slightly around the 24-metre-wide orchestra, giving the auditorium an almost horseshoe-like shape. About 150 stone seats on ten rock-cut steps are still in place on the south side of the auditorium. Dr Lindner estimates the theatre held between 500 and 800 spectators, with those in the upper seats enjoying the comfort of backrests built into the seats. On the north side, the auditorium is badly eroded, and only a few seats remain in the lower rows. Immediately across the wadi from the theatre are the remains of a large rectangular structure built from neatly cut stones.

The theatre at Sabra

At the level of the top row of badly eroded seats on the left (north) side of the auditorium, a thick channel carved out of the rock was probably originally covered by stone slabs or the seats themselves. The channel, which seems to have diverted water around the auditorium seats, is almost certainly related to the complex water gathering system that Dr Lindner investigated in the high cliffs above the theatre. Immediately above the top row of seats, in the centre of the auditorium, are the remains of a thick stone wall that still stands nine courses high. This wall formed a reservoir behind it, which was the lowest of four such installations at different levels in the cliffs directly above the theatre. The highest structure was a dam some 100 metres above the theatre, which collected rainwater from an adjacent mountain valley and directed it downhill via a series of channels. Between these upper and lower reservoirs were two intermediate ones that also trapped run-off rainwater and conserved it for use by the residents of Sabra throughout the dry season. The orchestra of the theatre itself may also have served as a reservoir, though this has yet to be verified.

For a distance of several hundred metres south of the theatre, the right bank of the Wadi Sabra is littered with the debris and architectural remnants of its Nabataean/Roman structures. Distinctive Nabataean capitals, column drums and bases are scattered throughout the area, along with considerable Nabataean/Roman pottery fragments and occasional stones with Nabataean inscriptions. About 200 metres south of the theatre, a small side wadi comes into Wadi Sabra from the right (west). On the north and south banks of this wadi stand wall remains of several buildings, including stacked tiles and a tile floor that may have been part of a kiln or baths complex. On the north bank, some 20 metres above the blue 'Wadi Sabra' sign, are the remains of what is thought to have been a Nabataean temple complex. Up the hill to the west are wall lines and many tumbled stones, some of which have plaster and Nabataean inscriptions on them.

Sabra lies at an altitude of some 775 metres above sea level, nearly 100 metres lower than the centre of Petra. This gives it a slightly milder climate, suggesting to some earlier scholars that it may have served as a Nabataean winter resort, where enjoyment of the mild weather may have been enhanced by the entertainment provided at the theatre. Where the Nabataeans actually lived remains unclear, but the temples and theatre suggest this may have been primarily a religious precinct, used for ceremonies but not inhabited throughout the year by a large permanent population.

After climbing back out of the Wadi Sabra, you can take a slightly different route back to the city centre through Ragbat al-Btahi, west through Ras Sleiman and Ragbat al-Barra, past the Snake Monument, and into the city via the Wadi Thugra.

As-Sa'adeh

About nine kilometres further south from Sabra is a site that is impossible for visitors to reach except on a two-day trip with a guide. This area is known as As-Sa'adeh and was briefly explored in 1983 by Zeidoun Muheisen and Maurice Gory. It has plentiful water all year round and still shows standing walls, cisterns, and a long stone canal. Pottery from the site dates from the Neolithic, Iron, Nabataean, Roman, Byzantine, and Islamic periods. Like Sabra and Braq, it was probably a caravan station on the route to Petra from the south.

Nebi Haroon

About two kilometres south-west of central Petra as the crow flies is the 1350-metre-high summit of Jabal Haroon, the highest peak in the Petra area. It is crowned by a small, domed mosque which local tradition says marks the burial place of the Prophet Aaron (Nebi Haroon, in Arabic), the brother of Moses. The spot is known to the local inhabitants of the Petra area as Nebi Haroon, or Jabal Haroon (Aaron's Mountain). Visitors should always remember that Nebi Haroon is revered as holy ground by the local inhabitants, and, with its ancient Islamic mosque (rebuilt at the end of the 14th century), it should be accorded the respect and decorum that are appropriate at places of worship throughout the world.

The long route can be difficult to follow in places, and there are few ancient monuments to see on the way, though the view from the summit is rather spectacular. There are places where the path passes over narrow ledges on the mountainside, so this trip should be made only with a local guide. The one-way trip to Nebi Haroon takes nearly two and a half hours from Qasr al-Bint, and all but the last 20 minutes can be done on horseback or donkey. At the foot of the last climb to the summit are the remains of a once barrel-roofed masonry reservoir.

Jabal Ma'iz

Near a small ravine on the east foot of Jabal Haroon, along the small tributaries that feed into the Wadi Wigheit between Jabal Haroon and Jabal al-Barra, is a 'sanctuary' area discovered and reported by Mr Peter Parr in 1960. Between the ravine and a small, isolated hill known as Jabal Ma'iz, is a 200-metre-long terrace with scattered remains of ancient Nabataean occupation, including walls, building stones, the odd column drum, typical Nabataean pottery, graffiti, at least one Dushara god block, and a one-metre-high relief carving of a seated but now headless female figure in a niche. Mr Parr points out the resemblance of this area to Sidd al-Ma'ajin and Qattar ad-Deir, as small, secluded sanctuaries, associated with water sources and full of graffiti, Dushara blocks, niches and other cultic or religious carvings. He notes: 'It is tempting to see in the Wadi Wigheit site a similar sanctuary; a place, if not of organised cult, then at least of popular reverence.'

116

GROUP 9

THE REGION OF AD-DEIR

It is best to visit Ad-Deir in the mid-to-late afternoon, when its facade is wondrously lit by the setting sun. This also permits an early afternoon ascent during warm weather, when most of the trail is shaded from the hot sun. The trip to Ad-Deir can be further enhanced by having the Petra Forum Hotel serve a full lunch in a Nabataean *triclinium* perched on the summit of a hill ten minutes beyond Ad-Deir, overlooking Wadi Araba to the west. The one-hour ascent to Ad-Deir through the Wadi ad-Deir, starting at the new Forum Restaurant, was the main processional route the Nabataeans used to reach Ad-Deir.

The Lion Triclinium

From the Forum Restaurant, head north in the Wadi ad-Deir through a narrow, sandy area with carved chambers on both sides of the path, including several tomb chambers to the left. After five minutes, several blue and white signs to the left mark the entrance to the short wadi, or ravine, of the Lion Triclinium (whose top is partly visible over the signs). It is best known for the two lions

The Lion Triclinium

carved in relief on either side of the doorway. Like the larger lion monument on the way up to the High Place of Sacrifice, these lions are thought to have represented an important Nabataean deity, perhaps the goddess Atargatis/Al-'Uzza. Its precise date is unknown. Interesting elements on its classical facade include the highly carved, decorated capitals of the corner pilasters, the horizontal frieze of alternating triglyphs and metopes with Medusa heads at both extremities (over the capitals), and a crowning, low-pitched pediment supporting three urns. Just to the left of the *triclinium* is a large Dushara block in a niche in the rock face. Further to the left, two small tombs with simple rectilinear carvings over the doorways seem earlier than the Lion Triclinium.

The Wadi Kharareeb Biclinium

From the Lion Triclinium, the Wadi ad-Deir path becomes a staircase, and after about a minute's walk you pass underneath a boulder that has fallen from the adjacent cliffs. Beyond the boulder, the path enters a flat, open area with two weathered tomb facades some 50 metres further on, to the right. As the Wadi ad-Deir turns west, the smaller Wadi Kharareeb comes in to meet it from the right (north). Some 200 metres into this wadi, carved into its right (east) cliff-face, is a *biclinium* with two interior benches reached by small staircases against the front wall. There

The Wadi Kharareeb Biclinium

is also a small grave towards the back, but this is a later addition. The facade has three urns over its pediment, a simple doorway, and well preserved Nabataean capitals over the compound (half-square, half-round) pilasters. The 15-minute detour to see this charming monument is well worth while.

Qattar ad-Deir
Return to the junction of Wadi Kharareeb and Wadi ad-Deir, and continue walking up Wadi ad-Deir as it travels west through a flat, open area and reaches a long, winding staircase. At the first big landing, where the steps make a sharp turn to the west, look up to the north into a wide, cavernous ravine. Leave the steps at the landing and climb towards the upper west reaches of this ravine, to visit Qattar ad-Deir. This is a dramatic ledge, some 50 metres long, sheltered beneath a rock overhang on the west side of the top of the ravine. The area has long been known as a holy spot because of the percolating water that drips into it all year round from the overhanging rocks. The word *qattar* derives from the Arabic verb meaning 'to drip'. There are, in fact, two such areas on the route to Ad-Deir, known respectively as Qattar al-Asfal (lower *qattar*) and Qattar al-Aa'la (higher *qattar*). This is Qattar al-Asfal, and is by far the more important of the two.

As you walk on to the ledge of the Qattar ad-Deir, you first pass a badly eroded door to your left that leads into a dark, humid and moss-covered *triclinium*, with three benches and a large chamber in its rear wall. Beyond the *triclinium* are many cultural and religious carvings on the cliff-face, including niches with pilasters, Dushara blocks, Nabataean inscriptions, deep niches, a cross, and a small basin with an outlet beneath. Just beyond these, and cut into the floor of the ledge, are four interconnected water tanks, each slightly higher than the next, to collect the dripping water from the hidden source in the overhanging rocks. On the rock-face above the last tank is a large, two-armed carved cross looking very much like a Cross of Lorraine, with a Nabataean inscription next to it.

The winding stairs in Wadi ad-Deir climb steadily towards the north-west, past a stone bench in a sharp turn in the staircase, and after several sharp turns, enter an open, shelf-like area from where you have a good view back towards the centre of Petra and the Royal Tombs. As you leave this area and pass through a short

Qattar ad-Deir

rock-cut corridor, high above to the north is your first glimpse of the top of the great urn above Ad-Deir.

Just on the other side of the little corridor is the so-called 'Hermitage', announced by a small sign along the side of the path. The Hermitage is the modern name, given on the strength of some crosses carved into the interior walls of a series of caves in the upper reaches of a rock outcrop to the right of the path.

Beyond the Hermitage, the path follows a deep ravine on the left (west) that has been romantically called Hermitage Gully, but is, in fact, the upper end of Wadi ad-Deir. Just before the path ascends a small staircase, about 20 metres before the upper end of the ravine and next to two trees, are niche-like cuttings on both sides of the upper faces of the wadi. These are thought to have held the springer stones of an arch, or bridge, that crossed the wadi, leading to an installation about 30 metres to the west composed of rock-cut pools, chambers and semicircles. This was called the 'Valley High Place' after its discovery in July 1905 by four professors from Beirut's Syrian Protestant College (later to become the American University of Beirut). Because of the many tombs in the area this 'high place' may have been more of a mortuary chapel. After a few more minutes of climbing, you pass through a short, rock-cut corridor into a wide open area, and the facade of Ad-Deir is around the corner to the right.

Ad-Deir

Ad-Deir, the 'monastery' or 'convent' in Arabic, boasts Petra's largest facade. It measures 50 metres wide by nearly 45 metres high, with an eight-metre-high doorway. The 10-metre-high urn at the top rests on a rare, free-standing Nabataean capital. Most scholars see Ad-Deir as a Nabataean temple, with a single internal chamber measuring approximately 12.5 by 10 metres. Carved out of the rear wall is a large, arched recess approached by two small flanking staircases. It would have held the stone block or other representation of the god worshipped here. Its date is unknown, though on stylistic grounds it is often dated to the mid-1st century AD. Dr Hammond suggests Ad-Deir may have been the unfinished tomb of one of the later Nabataean kings. Several small crosses scratched into the rear wall suggest Ad-Deir may also have been used as a place of worship by the Byzantine Christians of Petra after the early 4th century.

Architecturally, it has strong parallels with both the Khazneh and the Corinthian Tomb, but is a simpler, bolder expression of Nabataean style. Ad-Deir's composite (part round, part square) pilasters and capitals are particularly well preserved. The lower storey has a simple doorway flanked by six engaged pilasters, which in turn are flanked by two shallow niches with arched pediments and two more composite pilasters at the extremities. The two niches of the ground floor and the three of the upper may, as Mrs Crystal-M. Bennett has suggested, have been intended to house statues, such as those in the Roman Soldier Tomb and the Khazneh, in which case the ornamentation of Ad-Deir may never have been finished. The elaborate processional way to Ad-Deir from the city centre, and the vast, flat courtyard that was carved in front of it, suggest this was a site of large-scale ceremonies. Directly north of the courtyard are the remains of an ancient open-air altar reached by steps from the courtyard, and which may have been used in public ceremonies in the large area in front of Ad-Deir. From the altar, carved steps lead up to the urn on top of Ad-Deir.

There are many other installations throughout the vast area around Ad-Deir. The rocks directly facing it to the west are full of

Ad-Deir

carved chambers, tombs and platforms. Immediately visible a few hundred metres to the west is a square chamber in an elevated rock-face. This is well worth a visit, for it contains a beautiful, large (4 by 2-metre) niche in the shape of a pedimented doorway in its rear wall, unfortunately now covered with much modern graffiti. Carved on a simple platform is an 'inner' doorway, flanked by pilasters and topped by a horizontal run of alternating triglyphs and metopes. This inner doorway is flanked in turn by two more pilasters, each decorated with six rectangular panels and pedimented. Above each pilaster is a carved figure of a person dressed in a toga-like garment and carrying an object in one hand. The restricted open space in front of the niche chamber is covered with architectural fragments, including column bases and drums, suggesting to some scholars that a Roman temple may once have stood on this spot.

About a ten-minute walk north-west of Ad-Deir is a well preserved *triclinium* now used by the Petra Forum Hotel to serve lunches. It faces south, and is located on the south side of a rock promontory, in an area called Dangoor Ad-Deir. The door has two flanking pilasters, with a recessed arch cut into the rock. To the left of the doorway is a semicircular niche with a Dushara god block and a small platform beneath it, with two flanking pilasters. From this *triclinium*, you have spectacular views over Wadi Araba to the west.

From here you should walk to the cliff-face that extends some 150 metres north of Ad-Deir. The north end of this cliff-face leads into a small, enclosed wadi with a prominent rock overhang on its east side, and rock-cut steps on its left (west) side leading up to several platforms that look like altars. If you climb up on to the ledge beneath the rock overhang on the east side of the wadi and walk into it for about 30 metres, next to a cave opening is a half-metre-square niche surrounded by a carving of two men and their camels flanking a god block. The chamber to the left has a small Dushara block carved into a niche in the centre of the rear wall.

On the way back to Ad-Deir, you pass a series of rooms, niches and burial chambers carved into the rock-face to your left. The first room to the left has a splendid niche beneath a recessed lintel and a pediment, with another semicircular niche to its right.

GROUP 10

THE HIGH PLACE OF SACRIFICE AND WADI FARASA

The High Place of Sacrifice ('Al-Madbah' in Arabic) may have been the most important of Petra's many high places in Nabataean times. On the top of a promontory, 1036 metres above sea level and 200 metres above the city, the High Place is located on the summit of Jabal Madbah. Early western travellers noted as many as eight different approaches to the High Place, though two main routes are used today. It takes 25 minutes to reach the High Place of Sacrifice via the Wadi Mahafir, the fastest route starting near the Theatre, but nearly two hours to return from the High Place to the Qasr al-Bint via the Wadi Farasa route, because of the many monuments to see on the way down.

Just before the Theatre, a series of reconstructed steps leads off to the left, heading into the high, narrow Wadi Mahafir. You pass below a smooth, north-facing rock-face that was an ancient quarry, still showing several double rows of vertical 'footholds'. Leaving the quarry to the left, the path goes down some steps and passes through a corridor some 25 metres long, with faint remains of carved steps. It then passes through a level sandy area, and starts up a long series of staircases. After about ten minutes from the start of the trip, you make a sharp left turn and face up into a long, carved staircase and corridor, with the right wall completely covered with Nabataean tooling marks. The staircase is some 40 metres long, with a short corridor section in the middle. After ten more minutes, you cross the narrow top of the Wadi Mahafir to enter an open area where you can look up to the west and catch a first glimpse of one of the stone obelisks and a corner tower of the fort near the High Place. The path to the High Place is relatively easy to follow, but should you ever feel you are losing your way keep an eye out for the blue squares that have been painted along the route. After a few minutes, you pass a small stone bench to your left, underneath a big tree on the cliff-face. Above you are the two obelisks to the south, and the fort to the north. There is usually a Bdul family at the summit selling cold drinks, tea and water.

124

The Obelisks

The two great, mysterious obelisks near the High Place of Sacrifice were formed by painstakingly carving away the top of the rock ridge all around them, leaving two exposed cores that were worked into pyramid-like pillars. The quarrying technique used to hew away the surrounding mountain top is best seen from the fort to the north, on the other side of the gully that was also formed by quarrying away the natural rock. It is possible that the rock that was cut away to leave the obelisks was subsequently used to build the fort – if, as some have suggested, the fort, obelisks and High Place were all contemporary, though there is no firm evidence for this. The western obelisk, at seven metres high and 3.35 by 2.13 metres at its base, is slightly taller and fatter than its eastern twin, which is 6.4 metres high and 2 by 1.68 metres at the base.

The obelisks are thought to represent two Nabataean gods, perhaps their leading deities, Dushara and Al-'Uzza or Allat. There are several other examples of gods represented in twin pillars throughout the ancient Near East, attested to in the Bible,

The High Place Obelisks, with the Fort in the background

on coins, and from other sources. It is even possible, as Mrs Crystal-M. Bennett and others have suggested, that the High Place area was a holy sanctuary inherited by the Nabataeans from the Edomites before them. The Edomites' worship of male and female fertility gods may have been passed on to the Nabataeans along with their penchant for open high places. It is impossible to say if the obelisks relate to the High Place of Sacrifice itself, higher up on the north end of the same mountain. Another school of thought believes the twin obelisks may 'announce' the presence of the twin altars at the nearby High Place, which may have been dedicated to the worship of two gods.

The Fort at the High Place

From the obelisks, looking across the gully to the north, you see the remains of the fort's corner towers and walls that still stand in some places to over 20 courses of stone. Inside the fort, you can trace some of its east and west wall lines. The walls were often set into foundations in the bed-rock against the very edge of the mountain, making the fort difficult to assault and capture. Like the obelisks, the dating and purpose of this fort are still unknown, for it has never been properly studied. It has been called Nabataean, Roman, Byzantine and Crusader, but in the absence of excavations its original construction date must remain no more than an educated guess. If it was a lookout fortress to survey the exposed southern reaches of the city, it may have played this role during more than one period in Petra's history.

Dr Axel Knauf of Yarmouk University suggests the fort may have been a stately entrance, or *propylaeum*, to the High Place of Sacrifice, for the stones all show the typical Nabataean dressing and the walls appear too thin to have played a defensive role.

The High Place of Sacrifice

From the fort, climb over the smooth rocks to the north to reach the High Place of Sacrifice, carved out of the flat, almost oval summit of Jabal Madbah. The sanctuary is composed of a large central court with a raised platform, two altars, a pool, associated drains and other miscellaneous cultic installations. The central court is a 16 by 7-metre, sunken rectangle aligned almost exactly north–south, and sloping very slightly to the south. A shallow cutting formed a bench around three sides, in a typical Nabataean

The altars at the High Place, with the raised platform in the foreground

triclinium arrangement. Near the south-east corner, a 5.6-metre-long drain spills over the east edge of the summit. One metre south of the north-west corner, the staircase of nine rock-cut steps that enters the court marks the main approach to the High Place during Nabataean times. In the centre-left of the court, facing the altar, is a 1.55 by 85-centimetre platform that is 12.5 centimetres higher than the court. It may have been used by the priests or the congregation, held an idol or sacrificial offerings, or even served as a *mensa sacra*, or shewbread table that is common in biblical narratives.

If people or animals were actually sacrificed here, the ceremony took place at the main altar. This was a 3 by 2-metre, rectangular structure approached by several steps from the court. It stood one metre above the level of the court, and was surrounded on the north, west and south by a passageway that may have been used by the clergy for circumambulation. All but the south-west corners of the altar are cut down about 7.5 centimetres, perhaps to support a cover or ornamental devices for the altar. A 10-centimetre-deep hole carved into the top of the altar, as Dalman first suggested, may have held the Nabataean idol block or statue.

The High Place of Sacrifice (Al-Madbah) (*after G.L. Robinson*)

Less than a metre south of the main altar is the second altar, a 1.14-metre-wide circular basin composed of two concentric circles. It is carved out of the top of an outcropping of natural rock that was retained after the court and altar areas were formed. A drain from the smaller, deeper inner circle discharged on to the four steps that led up to it from the north. The 'round altar' was considerably larger than the main 'rectangular altar'. On its east edge, just below the concentric depressions, is a 1.55-metre-long cavity, or tank, carved into the bed-rock as it slopes towards the court, with a drainage hole cut into its south end. It has been suggested that the round altar was used for libations or for sacrifices, while the tank below it may have served to wash the sacred vessels used in the ceremonies.

About five metres south of the court is a rectangular pool with a small intake channel coming into its north-east corner, and a larger drainage channel exiting from its south-east corner, spilling over the east edge of the promontory. This pool provided the ample supply of clean water required for the ceremonies that took place here. The precise nature of those ceremonies is unknown today, though most Nabataean scholars feel that the ceremonies of ritual sacrifice that took place here probably used animals, not humans. The Nabataeans may have practised human sacrifice, however, to judge from a few literary references, including an inscription at Medain Saleh that reads: 'Abd Wadd, priest of Wadd, and his son Salim, and Zayd Wadd, have consecrated the young man Salim to be immolated to (the God) Dhu Gabat.'

Just over 100 metres to the north of the High Place, on a west-facing ledge opposite a lone tree, is the moon shrine a one-metre-square niche carved into a recessed rock-face, above a two-metre-wide ledge. It is composed of two rounded pillars with a crescent moon on top of each, flanking a central niche with a carved god block. Just a few metres to the north of the moon shrine is a broad, well preserved staircase forming part of the main Nabataean processional approach to the High Place from the north. This route to and from the High Place is difficult to negotiate today.

The descent from the High Place via Wadi Farasa

To return to the city centre via the Wadi Farasa route, go back down through the fort, walk south about 50 metres past the refreshments stand, through an area of bright bed-rock, then turn sharply to the right and start walking down a series of carved steps, staying close to the cliff-face to the right. After less than 100 metres, keep your eye open for a four-line Nabataean inscription carved in big letters into the base of the cliff-face to your right, behind a tree and just before a small staircase. Behind a bush on the right of the path, about ten minutes further on, is another fine two-line Nabataean inscription in light coloured letters on a black rock. The path then makes a sharp turn back to the south, and goes down a short staircase into a large open area.

The Medallion and Block Relief

About 50 metres in front of you and to the right, a circular rock platform with an overhang protrudes from the mountain, and hidden behind three small boulders on the circular platform is the lovely medallion and block relief. This 1.45-metre-high monument is composed of a niche with a carved Dushara block, with a slightly oval and concave framed medallion niche above it containing a carved but weathered human bust. Dr Hammond believes the medallion bust and the Dushara block were created together as an interrelated whole. He suggests the bust is that of a Nabataean goddess of grain or vegetation. The medallion and block relief may therefore represent an important stage in the transition of the Nabataeans' representations of their gods, first as stone blocks and later as anthropomorphic human figures. Dr Hammond suggests this monument may represent an intermediate stage in this evolution, when the chief male deity Dushara was still represented as a stone god block, while his accompanying female deity, either Allat or Atargatis/Al-'Uzza was already being represented in human form. If so, the monument may date from a period during or after the 1st century BC.

After a few moments, you reach a series of narrow steps with several Nabataean inscriptions on the dark face of the stone to your left. To the right is a good aerial view of the Roman Soldier Tomb far below. The path then passes through a short rock-cut corridor, to exit into a small terrace with two interesting monuments.

The Medallion and Block Relief

The Altar
Immediately after you leave the corridor, look back to your right to see, partly hidden behind a large bush, a two-metre-high, rock-cut altar. This is perhaps the best example of the many such cultic monuments that were placed along processsional routes to high places.

The Lion Monument
On the left of the open terrace is the rock-carved Lion Monument. The lion measures some five metres long, and is seen from its right, with its head facing out at a 90-degree angle. Its four legs, body and uplifted face are very clear. A carved channel above its head passed water through a pipe and out of the lion's mouth. There may once have been a basin to catch the water that flowed out of its mouth, or only a simple channel that connected with the rock-cut water channel alongside the steps leading down to the Wadi Farasa.

The Lion Monument probably served two purposes, one practical the other spiritual. The lion was often used to represent Nabataean deities, with various scholars suggesting it was the personification either of the main Nabataean god Dushara or of his female consort, Allat or Al-'Uzza. Its location along a major

The Lion Monument

route up to one of the most important Nabataean cultic centres, the High Place of Sacrifice, was meant to set the stage for the acts of worship that would follow at the end of the hard climb to the summit. Its practical role as a fountain must have been highly welcomed by the ascending worshippers, who could pause here for a few moments to rest and perhaps also quench their thirst.

Just as you leave the Lion Monument and start down the steep, winding staircase, you can trace the well preserved remains of a waist-high water channel cut out of the rock-face to the left. This carried the water that flowed out of the lion's mouth to a cistern at the foot of the staircase, at the head of the Wadi Farasa. After five minutes, at the bottom of the staircase, you enter a secluded little north–south wadi known as Wadi Farasa East. To your left, at the head of the wadi, a staircase leads into the cistern that received the water from the lion fountain. Follow the path on through the wadi for another two minutes, to reach the Garden Temple complex.

The Garden Temple complex

The Garden Temple complex is approached up a flight of seven steps on to a courtyard in front of the temple. It has a simple facade of two free-standing columns flanked by two engaged

The Garden Temple complex

columns, forming a portico *in antis*. Behind the columns is the interior shrine area. A small open area in front of the temple was thought to be a garden, and has given the monument its name.

Above the temple roof, on a natural terrace originally reached by a flight of now collapsed steps to the west of the temple facade, is a 5-metre-deep, plastered water cistern, 28 metres long and 5–6 metres wide. You reach the cistern over a cut staircase east of the temple, just beyond the impressive stone wall that held up the south side of the terrace. This huge cistern was one of the important water storage points in this part of the city. It was fed by local water channels as well as by a spur from the main channel that brought water into Petra from the Braq springs, four kilometres south of Petra. The Braq region, easily reached on the new paved road from Wadi Musa to Taiybeh and Rajif (six kilometres from the Petra Forum Hotel), still shows extensive evidence of the Nabataean water works, including pools, water channels, and the tumbled remains of many buildings. The extensive study of Petra's water system by Dr Zeidoun Muheisen of the Jordanian Department of Antiquities traced the main channel from Braq northwards, past the Lion Monument and the Theatre, to a distribution point along the north-west flank of Jabal Madbah that fed several secondary cisterns and channels. These channels were built of small ceramic pipe sections, and supplied water to several points in the city centre, including the 'baths' just south of the Arched Gate.

An S-shaped staircase with several landings leads into the south-west corner of the cistern, near a tree that has taken advantage of the cistern's still functioning water storage capacity. North of the cistern is a room that once had an arched roof. The roof itself has long disappeared, leaving only the carved slots from where the arches sprang. Twelve large niches are carved into this room's standing walls. Continuing down the path, you pass the Garden Temple to your right and walk down a long rock-cut staircase through a narrow crevice, sporting two wall niches at the bottom of the steps. At the end of the staircase, you reach the area of the Roman Soldier Tomb.

The Roman Soldier Tomb

The Roman Soldier Tomb was the focal point of an enclosed complex of monuments that included the *triclinium* opposite, and

The Roman Soldier Tomb

a now disappeared colonnaded portico around a central courtyard between the two. The tomb facade has two large engaged
columns flanked by corner pilasters with Nabataean-style
capitals. Across the top of the facade is a low-pitched pediment,
above which is an attic storey topped by a narrow terrace. Three
large niches across the centre of the facade housed badly
weathered statues that were each carved out of six stacked stone
blocks. The central statue is of a now headless figure dressed in
Roman military garb, perhaps a Roman soldier or legionary after
whom the tomb has been named. There are no inscriptions that
might help identify when or for whom the tomb was built,
though it is generally thought to date from the period after
Rome's annexation of Petra in AD 106.

In the main interior chamber are several segmented arched
burial recesses. Immediately above the upper right-hand corner
of the facade are five carved niches in a row. To the right of the
pediment is a peculiar relief carving in the cliff-face that looks like
a column and capital, on top of which are two god blocks. Above
and to the left of the five niches, a large horizontal cavity and a
smaller interior chamber are the remnants of a carved monument
that was defaced when the Roman Soldier Tomb was built.

There are several other carved installations immediately around the tomb, but not visible from the ground in front. These are best seen from the cistern terrace above the Garden Temple. To the left of the tomb, a few metres above the ground, is a rock boulder with a circular cutting and steps leading up to the platform above the tomb. More steps from the northern side of the platform lead to a ledge directly above a semicircular chamber along the cliff-face north of the tomb facade. There are four graves cut into this ledge, along with a niche and a chamber.

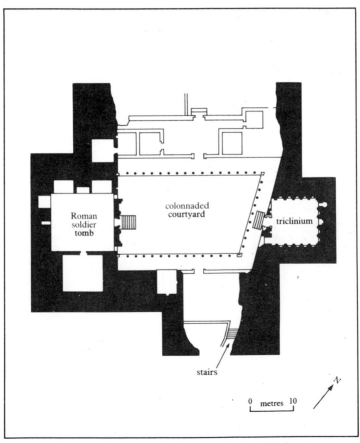

The Roman Soldier Tomb and Triclinium complex (*after W. Bachmann*)

The Triclinium

Opposite the Roman Soldier Tomb, at a slightly lower level, is a *triclinium* with the most spectacular interior of any monument at Petra. It has an unimpressive facade, except for a large semicircular niche with pilasters a few metres to its left. Inside, however, is an 11-metre-square chamber whose walls are each covered with six engaged, fluted half-columns carved out of the rock. In between the columns are five bays, each with a large vertical niche. The simple panel borders around the niches are best preserved on the inside of the front wall, flanking the main door. Decorative stones with simple mouldings inserted into grooves above the niches are still visible on the back and side walls. The best preserved columns and simple capitals are in the left rear (north-east) corner of the *triclinium*. The wide benches around the three walls are unusual in protruding so far from the walls.

The Nabataean inscription at the Turkmaniyya Tomb confirms that a *triclinium* and a tomb were often related to one another via a connecting courtyard and a colonnaded portico, to form a single complex that was usually reached by a main

The Triclinium

staircase. This is thought to have been the case here, with the *triclinium* being the funerary banqueting hall for those buried in the Roman Soldier Tomb opposite. The small area between the two monuments was levelled off into a terrace supported from the north by a retaining wall that still stands to eight courses of stone. A colonnaded portico ran around three sides of the courtyard, but not across the front of the Roman Soldier Tomb. Whether or not the installations of the Garden Temple complex were also part of the Roman Soldier Tomb and *triclinium* arrangement is uncertain.

As you leave the area of the Roman Soldier Tomb and the *triclinium* today, you pass through the low remains of a gateway threshold, down three steps, and over the remains of the retaining wall that once supported the north portico. On your right as you descend the path are the remains of a water channel cut into the cliff-face, and a niche with a grooved lintel. Some 25 metres after passing through the gateway remains and over some small staircases, you can take a brief detour to visit the collection of interesting monuments in Wadi Nmeir.

The Wadi Nmeir tombs

After leaving the Roman Soldier Tomb, turn left (west) in front of a well preserved staircase cut into the end of a small rock promontory, and head for the mouth of a small, enclosed wadi that is parallel to, but a few hundred metres west of, the Wadi Farasa, aiming for a cave in the distance with a wooden door over it. Some 40 metres into the Wadi Nmeir, beyond the remains of what seems to have been a small dam, are some facades cut into the rock-faces. About 25 metres past the dam, on the west cliff-face is a tomb that resembles the Roman Soldier Tomb, but without the upper level of the facade with the statue niches. Six deep burial *loculi* are carved high into the back wall of the single internal chamber, whose ground is littered with nicely carved decorative stones.

To the left (south) of this tomb is a squarish single chamber with faint signs of a carved doorway, and a big niche on the left internal wall. Next to it is another tomb whose classical door has eroded into a peculiar circular shape. The single internal chamber has three burial chambers high in the back wall, with part of the original blocking stone still in place in the central chamber.

Beyond this tomb, in the south-west corner of the wadi, are the remains of a cistern, with a channel feeding an adjacent pool.

To the east of the cistern, along the south face of the wadi, is a stunning but rarely visited little tomb with a carved interior that recalls the *triclinium* at the Roman Soldier Tomb. Its unimpressive facade has rondelles and triglyphs and a crowning pediment, with a totally eroded doorway and flanking corner pilasters. Inside, the rear wall has three deep burial cavities with floor graves, and five burial cavities in the left wall. Carved in relief on the smoothed rock face between the cavities are handsome pilasters with simple capitals. On the right wall, the six pilasters have been carved, but not the five burial chambers between them. After the *triclinium* at the Roman Soldier Tomb, this is Petra's most impressive interior.

The Renaissance Tomb

About 50 metres beyond the steps after the Roman Soldier Tomb is the elegant facade of the Renaissance Tomb, so named in the early 1970s by Iain Browning who thought 'the elegance of the doorway is so much like the work of the Italian Renaissance...'

The Renaissance Tomb

Crowning the two large engaged pilasters at the extremities of the facade are good examples of genuine Nabataean capitals. Along the top of the facade, the rather flattened pediment is surmounted by three urns, a motif that is repeated over the arch that spans the main doorway. This arch, carried over the doorway architrave on flanking pilasters and entablatures, gives the facade its unique, almost delicate look.

As you continue down the Wadi Farasa path, about 15 metres past the Renaissance Tomb an obelisk is carved in relief on the rock-face at eye level to your right.

The Broken Pediment Tomb

About 50 metres past the Renaissance Tomb, look sharply back to the right to spot the Broken Pediment Tomb on a raised recess facing north. The tomb, of uncertain date, gets its name from the broken pediment that dominates its otherwise tight facade. A staircase leads to a platform in front of the tomb, into which are cut two square and octagonal depressions that have been called 'tanks'. They probably related to ceremonies or rites that may have taken place here to commemorate those buried inside the

The Broken Pediment Tomb

tomb. The main tomb chamber connects from the inside with an adjacent chamber, both of whose doors still sport the notches that held their doors. Four recesses carved out of the wall towards the rear held the bodies of the dead, with indications that those responsible for the tomb never implemented plans to bury up to a dozen people in it. Along the right (west) wall, between low relief pilasters, panels mark the places where other *loculi* were supposed to have been carved out of the wall in the future, but never were. In the left (east) wall is a large arched recess.

About 40 metres after the Broken Pediment Tomb, you descend a small staircase next to a tree on the left side of the path. A handsome classical-style niche on the rock-face to the right is flanked by two small pilasters. Some 25 metres further on, there is a big chamber to the left with three niches on its outer wall, facing the path. Beyond it there is another large chamber, a former tomb, with three burial *loculi* in its back wall, and faint traces of a carved facade. To the east of these two chambers, across the path, is a chamber with a door and two windows above it, leading into a tomb chamber with *loculi*. Next to this former tomb, to the south, is the top of a tomb facade that broke off during an earthquake and collapsed in one piece on the wadi bed. A few moments further on, after passing some eroded tomb facades to the right, you reach the back of a blue sign that reads 'Farasa Valley'. To the right of the sign are the faint traces of another facade with a semicircular design over the door, similar to the Renaissance Tomb.

Look back up into the Wadi Farasa from here to appreciate the many tombs and other monuments carved out of the west face of Jabal Madbah, forming three or four tiers, or 'streets'. After the sign, follow the path straight ahead through a rocky area, heading in the general direction of Umm al-Biyara and Al-Habees mountains in the distance to the north-west. About five minutes after the 'Farasa Valley' sign, you pass over a slope with a line of tumbled stones that are the remnants of the south wall of the city.

The South City Wall

The path then leads straight through the remains of a small ancient gate in the wall, still identifiable by its lightly decorated corner stones in their original position in the ground. You can see the thick city wall heading for a short distance to the nearby cliff-face of Jabal Madbah to the east, and to the west in the direction of Umm al-Biyara and Al-Habees.

A survey in the mid-1960s by a British team headed by Peter Parr confirmed that only one southern wall ran almost in a straight line from the south-east foot of Al-Habees, through Al-Katutueh, south of Az-Zantur, and along the north ridge of Wadi Farasa, to terminate at the foot of the north-west cliff-face of Jabal Madbah. Much of it can be traced on the surface of the ground, with the best preserved stretch of 140 metres between Al-Katuteh and Jabal Madbah. To the west the wall remains are more fragmentary. Despite the substantial thickness of the wall line, this was not necessarily a fortified defensive structure, but may have served only as a boundary wall to delineate the city limits. The many other, smaller wall lines visible above the ground today are probably remnants of ancient terracing systems, large buildings or other civil or agricultural structures.

As you continue on the path to the north-west, the ground becomes increasingly littered with broken pottery fragments and the material debris of a distant civilisation. This is Al-Katuteh, a good place to pick up souvenir fragments of Nabataean pottery. Archaeologists interpret the heaps of broken pottery as representing the use of this area as a municipal dump shortly after the city fell under Roman control in the early 2nd century AD. After the small gate in the city walls, the path leads up to the summit of a hill from where you can see the Royal Tombs in the distance to the east. Keep walking towards the north-west, cross a small north–south wadi, and climb another hill to reach the rocky summit known as Az-Zantur, which the Horsefields saw as a fortified citadel. You can pass around the north or south side of Az-Zantur to reach Phar'oun's Pillar. Passing around the south side of Az-Zantur takes you past the Al-Katuteh excavations.

Phar'oun's Pillar

The solitary Phar'oun's Pillar, with its ten column drums, still stands next to the fallen segments of an identical adjacent column. It shows well the Nabataean technique of building columns of rather short and stumpy drums, in contrast with the larger, narrower drums of Greek and Roman architecture. Certainly, the columns were not always so isolated, for just behind them on the hillside to the east are the remains of a temple entrance, from which east–west wall lines and many tumbled stones climb the hill. Some have suggested that the obtuse angle of the back wall of the temple in Bachmann's 1921 plan of the area may have aligned with a main southern entrance to the city, linking the southern graves area at the mouth of the Wadi Thugra with the markets along the south side of the Colonnaded Street. The Nabataeans may have erected two pillars here to mark the approach to a holy area, in keeping with an ancient Middle Eastern tradition of using double pillars, or obelisks, to mark the entrance to a holy precinct. Could these twin pillars have served a similar function as the two obelisks near the High Place, as symbols of fertility gods that also marked the approach to an important cultic facility?

The Arabic name for the pillar is 'Zibb Phar'oun', or Pharaoh's phallus. This may have been somebody's idea of a joke on the early western travellers who visited Petra in the 19th century and constantly asked the local inhabitants the Arabic names of the monuments. If, however, the name reflects an ancient tradition, it could provide a link with both fertility symbols and Egyptian influences on the Nabataeans.

Al-Katuteh

The Horsfields dug at Al-Katuteh in the early 1930s to try to ascertain the path of the south city walls. A more extensive excavation was undertaken in 1958–9 by a British team under the leadership of Mr Parr and Dr Hammond. They dug an area adjacent to the original excavations of the Horsfields, about 100 metres south-west of Phar'oun's Pillar. The aim was to determine the history of the city by finding stratified occupation levels against the inner face of the city wall. The dig uncovered substantial sections of three-metre-high, half-a-metre-thick walls. These were not part of the south city walls, but rather belonged to a large building that measured over 18 metres long and five metres wide, aligned in a north-east/south-west direction. In fact, the excavators believe they have uncovered only the south-west corner of a much more substantial complex.

A courtyard connects through a door to a small annexe to the south-west, probably a later addition. Several side walls divide the main building into four-metre-square rooms that do not appear to be connected by doors. Buttress-like projections from the side walls held up the roof or perhaps even a second storey. The existing walls, still standing to 12 courses of stone, are rebuildings of earlier walls. Much moulded and painted wall plaster was recovered, indicating that the original building must have been quite a well decorated structure, perhaps a public building or the house of a wealthy merchant. Its precise date and function remain unknown.

It was most likely first built in its present form in the first half of the 1st century AD, on a spot that had been occupied for hundreds of years before. A deep excavation trench revealed the presence of earlier walls and a total of five metres of occupational debris beneath the floor lines of the Nabataean building. Mr Parr deduces from the excavated coins that the building was in use at the end of the 1st century AD and through the Roman annexation of AD 106, but probably went out of use soon after. It may be that during the rebuilding of the city after 106 this area was used as a municipal rubbish dump, accommodating the debris that was cleared out of the centre of Petra. (The word Katuteh in Arabic means 'dump' or 'rubbish heap'.) Most of the pottery on the surface of the ground seems to be from the 1st and 2nd centuries AD.

West Katuteh

About 75 metres west of Phar'oun's Pillar, near the base of Al-Habees, is the West Katuteh area excavated in 1981 by Dr Nabil Khairy of the University of Jordan, in co-operation with the Jordanian Department of Antiquities. Three adjacent excavated areas revealed intermittent Nabataean/Roman/Byzantine occupation, from the early 1st century AD to the mid-6th century.

The main feature of the site today is a 15 by 15-metre paved terrace oriented in the same direction as Qasr al-Bint, and perhaps also serving a religious purpose. The pavement rests on a podium in which there are several water installations or channels, three of which were excavated and can still be seen today. Channel A, at the north-east corner of the terrace, is the longest, widest and deepest of the three, measuring at least 3.2 metres deep at its north end. A groove cut along its upper reaches once held stones which supported a vaulted roof. Dr Khairy sees the channels as Nabataean reservoirs which stored and distributed water to the

144

immediate vicinity.

South of the paved terrace is an architectural complex of at least two rooms, while two staircases connect the terrace with a slightly higher paved area to the east of these rooms. Between the main paved terrace and the two rooms are the remains of base foundations, column bases and square plinths. These are thought to mark off the main entrance to the paved terrace, which Dr Khairy suggests was a *temenos*, or sacred enclosure, served by the architectural complex to the south. The *temenos* and the water cisterns seem to date from the Nabataean period, perhaps as early as the reign of Aretas IV and his second wife Shuqailat (AD 18–40).

East of the paved terrace is the six-metre-diameter apse of a Byzantine church from the second and third quarters of the 6th century. The apse was built of former Nabataean capitals that were each cut into four pieces, with the smooth face of the stone facing into the church and the floral decorations of the former capitals facing the wall, away from the view of the worshippers. Perhaps, Dr Khairy suggests, this was done 'to conceal any evidence of an earlier pagan worship which would be in conflict with Christian belief'.

Next to the apse of the church was a 4.15-metre-long paved area of small hexagonal slabs, dated by coins from the reign of Aretas IV before he married Shuqailat (9 BC–AD 18). A staircase of 11 steps on the south side of the pavement leads to the top of a naked sandstone rock. There is also a small basin north of the hexagonal pavement, which may have been used during ceremonies that took place here at the height of the Nabataean era. A few metres to the south-east, the excavations uncovered a Nabataean dwelling room that produced a rich collection of artefacts, including pottery, lamps, and coins dating from the first half of Aretas IV's reign, the same period that the large paved terrace and cisterns were in use. Particularly valuable were the 48 complete or fragmentary excavated Nabataean lamps, including a rare pottery lantern from the reign of Malichus II (AD 40–70).

After the initial Nabataean use of this area as a *temenos* in the late 1st century BC and throughout the entire 1st century AD, it seems to have been abandoned for about 150 years. It was re-used in the late Roman era, during the second half of the 3rd century but abandoned again between the late 3rd century and the mid-6th century. The Byzantine church was built, and the former Nabataean *temenos* remodelled, in the second and third quarters of the 6th century. Thereafter the site seems to have been used heavily for around a generation, before finally being abandoned for good.

Jabal Nmeir

Nearly a kilometre south-west of Jabal Madbah and the High Place of Sacrifice, Jabal Nmeir has a rock-cut staircase of 800 steps rising sharply from the bed of the Wadi Nmeir, which flanks Jabal Nmeir from the east. The staircase is interrupted twice by two terraces. Near the staircase at the upper terrace is the nearly half-metre-high carved figure of a Roman soldier. Further up the ascent is a carved room opposite a cistern, and near the summit there is a once-vaulted cistern. You can reach the Wadi Nmeir by walking south from the Wadi Farasa, or south over the hills from west of the obelisks at the High Place of Sacrifice. In 1929, the Horsfields saw Jabal Nmeir as a strategic lookout post overlooking the southern routes into Petra, and in direct signal contact with the fort near the High Place of Sacrifice.

GROUP 11

AL-WU'EIRA, SIQ AL-BARID AND BEIDHA

Al-Wu'eira Crusader Fortress

Al-Wu'eira, built sometime between 1108 and 1116, was the main Crusader fortress in the area of Petra the Crusaders knew as La Vallée de Moise or Le Vaux Moise (the Valley of Moses). It was considerably bigger and more complex than the smaller fortress on the summit of Al-Habees, and accommodated a permanent garrison, whose troops rotated duty at Al-Habees and perhaps other small lookout posts in the vicinity. Al-Wu'eira has never been studied in detail or excavated.

The fortress is perched on the summit of Jabal Wu'eira, surrounded by the Wadi Sh'ab Qais to the west and steep gorges

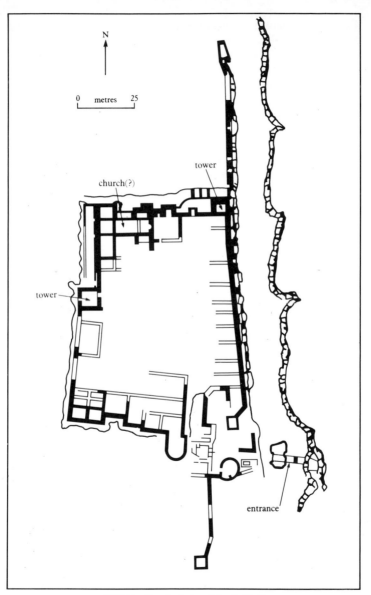

N

0   metres   25

church(?)

tower

tower

entrance

Al-Wu'eira Crusader Fortress (*after A. Musil*)

on the other three sides. Its main entrance was over an artificial bridge spanning a deep moat at its south-east corner. It leads into a roughly rectangular fortress with traces of rooms on all sides. A defensive wall with low battlements also extends beyond the main fortress to the north, from its north-east corner tower. Along the south wall are the remains of an apsed structure that may have been the church of the fortress. Scattered over the sprawling ruins are traces of arches, rooms, fortification walls, towers, vaulted chambers, cisterns, staircases and doorways. To the west of the fortress are remains of Nabataean installations, particularly several rock-cut staircases.

Siq al-Barid

Like Sabra to the south, Siq al-Barid was a self-contained 'suburb' or satellite community of Petra. You reach Siq al-Barid by car in ten minutes on a paved road that goes north from the Visitors' Centre, past Wu'eira fortress and the Bdul village. In antiquity, several tracks connected Siq al-Barid with the north Petra basin, and all along the wadis and plains between Petra and the Barid/ Beidha region are traces of structures such as cisterns, watchtowers, tombs, high places, niches, and water channels. The area is called Siq al-Barid because one enters the area of the monuments through a 35-metre-long fissure in the rocks that is a miniature of the great Siq at Petra. In fact, Siq al-Barid is itself a diminutive version of Petra, often called 'little Petra' by Jordan's foreign community.

When the paved road reaches a T-junction, turn left and travel about 800 metres to the entrance of Siq al-Barid. Two hundred metres after the junction, carved into the cliff-face to the right of the road, is an enormous Nabataean cistern, now sheltered behind a modern staircase and wall and still used by the area's inhabitants. On the other side of the road, an isolated rock full of carved channels and steps also has a large cistern on its south side. In the north rock-face of the open area in front of the entrance to Siq al-Barid is a lovely Nabataean classical monument, reached by a small staircase and with a single plain chamber inside. Like the Khazneh, it has been called both a tomb and a temple. The entrance of the little Siq was once controlled by a gate, whose sockets are still visible.

Emerging from the west end of the Siq, you enter the first

The temple at Siq al-Barid

open area full of rock-cut monuments of different kinds, some several storeys high, and remains of many staircases. On the left (south) cliffs is a large temple with a rather simple facade of corner pilasters flanking two free-standing columns, all with Nabataean capitals. About another 100 metres into Siq al-Barid is the second open area with many monuments and water installations. As you enter this area, you pass three fine *triclinia* to your right, each flanked by carved pilasters. Facing the third *triclinium* from the left side of the path is another large *triclinium* reached by a carved staircase of four steps. Further to the left is a fine carved staircase, and a few metres beyond it in the left (south) cliff-face is the famous *biclinium* with the remains of a painted ceiling fresco. The ancient staircase leading up to it has been rebuilt by the Department of Antiquities, and the inner chamber with the frescoes has been fenced off to protect the frescoes while still providing access for visitors. The *biclinium* has two benches or platforms along its east and west walls, leading into an arched recess in the rear wall whose ceiling was plastered and painted. On the walls of the *biclinium* are remains of stucco that was painted in yellow and red to resemble masonry panels. The vaulted ceiling once had a medallion in the centre, but this has long disappeared.

The ceiling fresco was a tapestry-like painting that included vines, flowers, seated and flying birds and at least three mythological figures – a seated Pan playing his flute, an Eros drawing his bow, and perhaps a winged Eros astride an eagle. Scholars such as the Horsfields dated the Siq al-Barid painting to around 30–20 BC. Others, such as Nelson Glueck, prefer to date it to the late 1st/early 2nd century AD, while recognising that the work could fit into a Mediterranean cultural and artistic tradition spanning several centuries. Carved into the west rock-face overlooking the threshold of the *biclinium* is a diminutive niche with a Dushara god block measuring just a few centimetres high.

On the summits of the cliffs surrounding Siq al-Barid are the remains of elaborate water catchment and storage systems, and several installations that have been called high places. The easiest high place to reach is in the third open area within the Siq al-Barid, 50 metres beyond the *biclinium*. Just as you enter this area, behind a tree to your right, a carved staircase of 33 steps leads up to the high place. At the west end of Siq al-Barid the surrounding cliffs narrow again, and a rock-cut staircase leads up through a narrow gap to a small natural terrace. This overlooks a vista to the west of hills, mountains and valleys, ultimately leading down to the Wadi Araba. From the Siq at the east end to this terminal staircase at the west, the Siq al-Barid area is about 350 metres long, and can easily be visited in an hour.

The prevalent theory about Siq al-Barid sees it as a caravanserai, where the camel caravans that came to trade at Petra stopped to do business and to rest before completing their journeys. There are at least six different tracks that link the Petra highlands with the Wadi Araba to the west. The easiest to negotiate was the route linking the Beidha/Barid area with Bir Mathkoor in the foothills of the Wadi Araba, from where several land routes led to Gaza and Alexandria. The many different shaped chambers inside Siq al-Barid included homes, offices, store-rooms, cisterns, temples, *triclinia*, tombs, cultic installations and other facilities.

Beidha

The excavated Stone Age village of Beidha, one kilometre south-west of Siq al-Barid on a dirt track, takes you back 9000 years in time. Beidha ('white' or 'the white one' in Arabic) dates from the period at the end of the Stone Age known as the Neolithic era, when people in the Near East were making the slow, gradual transition from small groups of nomadic hunter–gatherers to settled villagers who domesticated animals and cultivated plants. It was excavated by Mrs Diana Kirkbride during eight seasons between 1958 and 1983. Her excavations showed that Beidha flourished for at least 500 years around 7000–6500 BC, in the period known as the Pre-Pottery Neolithic B, or PPNB. There is evidence, in the form of campsites and semi-permanent hut shelters with hearths and post-hole areas, of earlier Neolithic people living on the spot before the PPNB village was established. There are also some excavated stone-lined pits, beads, stone tools and large hearths dating from the even earlier Natufian period, in the 9th and 10th millennia BC.

Mrs Kirkbride has identified six different stages of architectural development, during the 7th millennium BC, which can still be picked out from the excavation trenches. The first level, from around 7000 BC, has the remains on the west side of the dig of circular, single-room, houses with post-holes evenly spaced every 30–50 centimetres along the insides of the walls to hold wooden posts which supported the roof. The second level, from around 6800, also had circular houses with plastered floors and walls. The third level, from around 6700, shows ancient Beidha's finest construction work, typically rectangular houses with curving walls and rounded corners, plastered floors and walls, and internal fireplaces. The fourth and fifth levels, from around 6600, had typically large, single-room houses with plastered interiors entered by descending three steps. This period also had smaller, rectangular houses divided into six small rooms by thick, unplastered internal walls. Specialised artefacts discovered in these 'corridor houses' suggest they were craft workshops rather than dwellings. The badly eroded sixth level, from 6500–6000, shows remains of small rectangular houses with plastered floors.

Some 50 metres east of the village is a small PPNB 'sanctuary' area with peculiar basins, large standing stone slabs, and paved enclosures that defy categorisation. There are dozens of stone grinding querns scattered on the ground near the village, testifying to early man's first experiments with cultivating and grinding wheat and barley.

Chronology of Nabataean kings

BC

332   Alexander the Great conquers the land of Syria/Jordan.

312   First historical reference to Nabataeans, in Diodorus' accounts of
       clashes between Nabataeans and the forces of Antigonus, the
       Seleucid/Hellenistic ruler of Syria.

c.170/168   King Aretas I mentioned in inscription on Petra–Gaza road;
       biblical reference in Maccabees mentions 'Aretas, the prince of
       the Arabians'.
            A King Rabbel I may have reigned in second half of 2nd
       century.

c.100   Reign of King Aretas II, mentioned by the historian Josephus as
       'Aretas, King of the Arabians'.

c.93–85   King Obodas I (son of Aretas II).

86–62   King Aretas III ('the Philhellene'), son of Obodas I, expanded
       Nabataean kingdom and ruled Damascus for nearly 15 years.
            A King Obodas II may have reigned around 62–58.

64   Roman General Pompey captures Damascus and creates Roman
       Province of Syria.

62–30 or 58–30   King Malichus I.

30–9   King Obodas II.

AD

9 BC–AD 40   King Aretas IV ('the lover of his people').

40–70   King Malichus II.

70–106   King Rabbel II ('who brought life and deliverance to his people').

106   Emperor Trajan annexes Petra/Nabataea to Roman Empire, as
       part of new Province of Arabia with capital at Bostra.

130   Emperor Hadrian visits Petra.

Selected Bibliography

Books

Bowersock, G., *Roman Arabia*, Harvard University Press, Cambridge, Mass., and London (1983).

Browning, I., *Petra*, Chatto & Windus, London (1982).

Glueck, N., *The Other Side of the Jordan*, American Schools of Oriental Research, Cambridge, Mass. (1970).

— *Deities and Dolphins*, Strauss and Giroux, New York (1965).

Hammond, P., *The Nabataeans — Their History, Culture and Archaeology*, Paul Astroms Forlag, Gothenburg (1973).

Harding, G.L., *The Antiquities of Jordan*, Lutterworth Press and Jordan Distribution Agency (1967).

Kennedy, Sir A., *Petra, its History and Monuments*, Country Life, London (1925).

Lindner, M. (ed.), *Petra und das Königreich der Nabatäer*, Delpsche Verlagsbuchhandlung, Munich (1970).

— *Petra. The Guide through the Antique City*, Grafische Werkstätte Graf, Fürth (1985).

Lyttelton, M., *Baroque Architecture in Classical Antiquity*, Thames and Hudson, London (1974).

Murray, M., *Petra, the Rock City of Edom*, Blackie, London (1939).

Musées Royaux d'Art et d'Histoire, *Inoubliable Petra, Le Royaume Nabatéen aux confins du desert*, Brussels (1980).

Musée de Lyon, *Un royaume aux confins du désert: Petra et la Nabatène*, (1978).

Robinson, G.L., *The Sarcophagus of an Ancient Civilisation, Petra, Edom and the Edomites*, Macmillan, New York (1930).

Shahid, I., *Rome and the Arabs, A Prolegomenon to the Study of Byzantium and the Arabs*, Dumbarton Oaks Research Library and Collection, Washington, D.C. (1984).

Articles, Monographs, Reports and Dissertations

Bartlett, J.B., 'From Edomites to Nabataeans: A Study in Continuity,' *PEQ* 111 (1979) pp. 52–66.

—— 'The Rise and Fall of the Kingdom of Edom,' *PEQ* 104 (1972) pp. 26–37.

Bennett, C-M., 'Petra,' *Art International*, Vol. XXVI/1 (January-March 1983) pp. 2–38.

—— 'Fouilles d'Umm el-Biyara,' *RB* (1966) pp. 372–403.

Cleveland, R.L., 'The Conway High Place: Discovery, Excavation and Description,' *AASOR* XXXIV–XXXV (1960) pp. 57–78.

Dalman, G., 'The Khazneh at Petra,' *Annual of the Palestine Exploration Fund* (1911) pp. 95–107.

Glueck, N., 'A Nabataean Mural Painting,' *BASOR* 141 (February 1956) pp. 13–22.

Hamarneh, S.K., 'The Role of the Nabataeans in the Islamic Conquests,' *SHAJ* I (1982) pp. 347–50.

Hammond, P., 'Cult and Cupboard at Nabataean Petra,' *Archaeology* 34.2 (1981) pp. 27–34.

—— 'The Excavation of the Main Theatre at Petra, 1961–62, Final Report,' *Colt Archaeological Institute*, London (1965).

—— 'The Medallion and Block Relief at Petra,' *BASOR* 192 (1968) pp. 16–21.

—— 'The Crusader Fort on El-Habis at Petra, its Survey and Interpretation,' research monograph no. 2, University of Utah Middle East Center, Salt Lake City, Utah (1970).

Horsfield, G. and A., 'Sela-Petra, the Rock of Edom and Nabatene,' *QDAP* VII, VIII and IX (1938, 1939 and 1942).

Khairy, N., 'A New Dedicatory Nabataean Inscription from Wadi Musa,' *PEQ* (January–June 1981) pp. 19–26.

—— 'Some Aspects of the Byzantine Period from the 1981 Petra Excavations,' paper presented at the *4th Conference on the History of Bilad al Sham*, University of Jordan, Amman (October 1983).

Kirkbride, D., 'A Short Account of the Excavations at Petra in 1955–56,' *ADAJ* IV–V (1960) pp. 117–22.

Lindner, M., 'An Archaeological Survey of the Theatre Mount and Catchwater Regulation System at Sabra, South of Petra, 1980,' *ADAJ* 26 (1982) pp. 231–42.

155

Milik, J.T., 'Une inscription bilingue nabatéenne et greque à Petra,' *ADAJ* 21 (1976) pp. 143–54.

Milik, J.T and **Starcky, J.**, 'Inscriptions récemment découvertes à Petra,' *ADAJ* 20 (1975) pp. 111–30.

Muheisen, Z., 'L'alimentation en eau de Petra,' PhD dissertation, University of Paris (1983).

Negev, A., 'The Nabataeans and the Provincia Arabia,' *Aufstieg und Niedergang der Romischen Welt*, Vol. II.8, Berlin and New York (1977) pp. 520–686.

Parr, P., 'The Capital of the Nabataeans,' *Scientific American* 209 (1963) pp. 95–102.

— 'The Investigation of Some "Inaccessible" Rock-Cut Chambers at Petra,' *PEQ* (1968) pp. 5–15.

— 'Excavations at Petra 1958–59,' *PEQ* (1960) pp. 124–35.

— 'Recent Discoveries in the Sanctuary of the Qasr Bint Far'un at Petra,' *ADAJ* 12–13 (1967–8) pp. 5–19.

— 'La date du Barrage du Siq à Petra,' *RB* 74 (1967) pp. 45–9.

— 'Le "Conway High Place" à Petra, une nouvelle interpretation,' *RB* (1962) pp. 64–79.

Parr, P., Atkinson, K.B. and **Wickens, E.H.**, 'Photogrammetric Work at Petra, 1965–68: An Interim Report,' *ADAJ* 20 (1975) pp. 31–45.

Peters, F.E., 'The Nabataeans in the Hawran,' *Journal of the American Oriental Society* 97 (1977) pp 263–77.

Quantrill, M., 'An Architecture of Particular Inclination, Some Notes on the Nabataean Monuments at Petra,' *Art International* Vol. XXVI/1, (January–March 1983) pp. 39–45.

Starcky, J., 'The Nabataeans: A Historical Sketch,' *BA* Vol. XVIII (1955,4) pp. 82–107.

— 'Nouvelles steles funeraires à Petra,' *ADAJ* X (1965) pp. 43–9.

Wright, G.R.H., 'The Khazne at Petra: A review,' *ADAJ* VII and VIII (1962) pp. 24–54.

— 'Petra, the Arched Gate, 1959–60,' *PEQ* (1961) pp. 124–35.

— 'Structure of the Qasr Bint Far'un. A Preliminary Review,' *PEQ* (1961) pp. 8–37.

Zayadine, F., 'Recent Excavations at Petra,' *ADAJ* 26 (1982) pp. 365–94.

— 'Excavations at Petra, 1976 and 1978,' *ADAJ* 23 (1979) pp. 185–97.

— 'A New Commemorative Stele at Petra,' *Perspective* 12 (1971) pp. 57–73.

Abbreviations

AASOR   Annual of the American Schools of Oriental Research
ADAJ   Annual of the Department of Antiquities of Jordan
BA   Biblical Archaeologist
BASOR   Bulletin of the American Schools of Oriental Research
PEQ   Palestine Exploration Quarterly
QDAP   Quarterly of the Department of Antiquities of Palestine
RB   Revue Biblique
SHAJ   Studies in the History and Archaeology of Jordan, I

Glossary

acroterion: ornament at apex or outer angles of pediment
adyton: inner shrine or sanctuary of temple
architrave: lowest of three main parts of entablature
cella: main body of temple, containing cult image
Corinthian: one of the 'orders' of classical architecture based on a column
      type; developed from Ionic order
cornice: crowning and projecting element of entablature
crow-step: stepped, V-shaped motif, common on Nabataean tombs
Ionic: architectural order, preceding Corinthian
loculus: recess in tomb, holding sarcophagus
metope: space between triglyphs in Doric frieze, often decorated
pediment: gable above portico
pilaster: shallow rectangular column projecting from wall
stele *(plural: stelae)***:** commemorative carving, often pyramidal in shape
temenos: sacred precinct or enclosure
tholos: round building or section of building, usually surrounded by
      columns
triclinium *(plural: triclinia)***:** room with three benches, thought to be
      funerary banqueting hall, but also used for domestic purposes. A
      biclinium has only two benches.
triglyph: block with two vertical grooves, alternating with metopes to
      form a Doric frieze

Index

158

160

The Greater Petra Region

(after Derek Kennet)

1 Beidha
2 Siq al-Barid
3 Ad-Deir
4 Northern city walls
5 Southern city walls
6 Theatre
7 Khazneh
8 Sabra
9 Braq
10 Al-Madras
11 Wadi Musa village
12 Tawilan
13 Petra Forum Hotel
14 Al-Wu'eira Crusader Fortress
15 Nebi Haroon

The topographical and archaeological information in the endpaper maps is derived from a 1:2500 scale map (10m. contour interval with respect to an arbitrary datum) prepared by and copyright of Department of Photogrammetry and Surveying, University College, London, and Petra Excavation Fund, 1970. The publishers take full responsibility for any inaccuracies which may have arisen as a result of redrawing.

N
↑

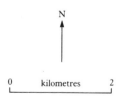

0   kilometres   2

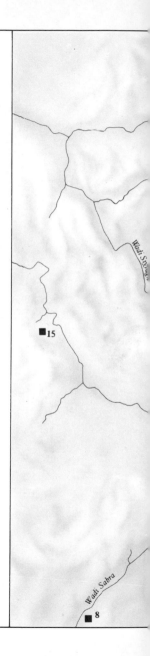